Teaching North American English Pronunciation

A Brief Introduction
with Photocopyable Handouts

Raymond C. Clark
and
Richard Yorkey

PRO LINGUA ⬤ ASSOCIATES

Pro Lingua Associates, Publishers

P.O. Box 1348
Brattleboro, Vermont 05302 USA
Office: 802-257-7779
Fax: 802-257-5117
Orders: 800-366- 4775
Email: info@ProLinguaAssociates.com
WebStore www.ProLinguaAssociates.com
SAN: 216-0579

At Pro Lingua
our objective is to foster an approach
to learning and teaching that we call
interplay, the **inter**action of language
learners and teachers with their materials,
with the language and culture,
and with each other in active, creative
and productive **play**.

ISBN 13: 978-0-86647-326-2; 10: 0-86647-326-2

This book is full of verse, much of it written by the authors, most of it humorous, a lot of it either in the public domain or from the folk tradition. Some of the Mother Goose rhymes and the limericks have been tweaked for pedagogical purposes. "Misquotes" may thus be assumed to be purposeful. The adaptations of scenes from *Plays for the Holidays*, © 2006 by Anne Siebert, were done by Ray Clark with permission.

This book was designed by Raymond C. Clark and Arthur A. Burrows. It was set in Cambria, a typeface designed by Jell Bosma, a Dutch typographer, in 2004, in collaboration with Steve Matteson and Robin Nicholas. Their objective was to develop a typeface that was easily legible on screen and yet would be handsome printed in a range of sizes. It is a serif font, both graceful and very evenly proportioned, which makes it easy to read even when the graphically somewhat complicated text is photocopied for use as handouts. Cambria has been sold with a variety of Microsoft products since 2007. This book was set by Arthur A. Burrows and printed and bound by McNaughton & Gunn in Saline, Michigan.

Printed in the United States of America
Second edition, first printing 2011. 1,200 copies in print.

Contents

Foreword

Part One of this book is largely the effort of Ray Clark. Part Two is based on the work of Richard Yorkey, a well-known figure in the world of TESOL for many years. Dick died recently, but before his death he discussed the possibility of Pro Lingua publishing his booklet, *American English Pronunciation Practice*, originally developed at the American University of Beirut in 1967, and privately published by Dick in 1991.

In the 1991 printing, Dick stipulated that: "Any part of this book may be reproduced or transmitted in any form, or by any means, electronic or mechanical including photocopying, recording, or by an information storage or retrieval system, with the full permission, personal happiness, and professional satisfaction of the author."

At the same time, Dick also offered his 1991 version to Pro Lingua. With his death his manuscript lay dormant until Ray Clark, taking Dick at his word, began to use selected pages as handouts in a variety of teacher training workshops and courses. They proved to be useful, and Ray began to develop additional material to accompany the handouts. Little by little, Ray's material took shape as what is now Part One of this book. It is essentially a simplified introduction to English phonology for practicing teachers who do not need or want a semester-long course. It is correlated with Dick's Part Two, described above as a pronunciation practice booklet for English language learners.

We are pleased that this revision of Dick's 1967 booklet will be used by English language learners in the second decade of the twenty-first century. As a creative and tireless contributor to our profession, Dick, too, would be pleased.

Introduction

This book is for the person who is helping a learner of North American English develop and improve their pronunciation. Part One introduces the basics of English phonology with reference to the writing system that represents it. Part Two is a collection of photocopyable handouts that can be used to help English language learners of all ages from the high beginning to advanced proficiency level.

In Part One, Section One is about the part of the phonological system called the segmental phonemes.* Essentially these phonemes represent the individual sounds of the language: the vowels and consonants. Section Two is about the suprasegmental aspects of the phonological system: in essence, stress, intonation, linking, and phrasing.

Part Two is a collection of photocopyable worksheet handouts. Although the teacher may serve as the model for the various practices, using the CDs will give the learners additional voices to listen to. Learners could use Part Two as a self-study guide by using the CDs.

For the teacher, using the two parts of the book can be a "Teach as you learn, learn as you teach" professional development experience in a face-to-face classroom context with learners, or the book can be used as a self-study course. The latter learning experience would definitely be enhanced by the use of the CDs.

There is a brief appendix that includes problem areas for different learners of English, and a compilation of phonetic alphabets.

---

* A phoneme is actually a class of sounds that are very similar to each other, but are actually slightly different physically. For example, the phoneme /P/, when it is actually spoken, will have different sound, depending on whether it is the first consonant in a word, in the middle of a word, or at the end of a word. Compare *pal, apple,* and *lap.* A phoneme, therefore, is strictly speaking not a physical sound but a collection of similar sounds that share common physical properties that are distinct from those of all other phonemes.

Preface:
The Goal and the Challenge

Human babies are born with the ability to produce a very wide variety of sounds. As they grow and develop, the sounds of their nurturers gradually become their sounds, and as they become speakers of a language, they acquire a sound system that includes only part of the sounds available to the new-born baby. As a second-language learner tries to acquire another, different sound system, one of the challenges they face is that they will tend to use the sound system they already have, and they may develop a very heavy accent. For example, a learner may have an "r" sound in their own language, but it is not the same sound as an English "r." Consequently, the learner may have a tendency to use their own "r" instead of the English "r" and they are misunderstood, or perhaps just sound "funny."

Learners of English are faced with many challenges, including the ability to learn new sounds and to produce the sounds of English with reasonable accuracy, and although good pronunciation is obviously important, it is neither necessary nor realistic for learners to be able to produce perfect "native speaker" English. The goal is to be understood by people who speak any one of the world's Englishes.

In fact, there is no official and "correct native speaker" pronunciation of English. In addition to the existence of several national varieties of English, the "North American" English of this book's title is also a variety of English. To be sure, Canadians and Americans do not have great difficulty in understanding each other's pronunciation, but every teacher and learner using this book should keep in mind and remind themselves that there are minor differences in pronunciation from one corner of North America to another and even among individual native speakers.

Part One
Introduction
to English Phonology

The Vowels

Learning a new vowel system can require the learner to modify vowels they already have and to develop new ones. This is especially true of the vowel system of English because English uses an uncommonly large number of vowels. In this book we will identify 16 different vowels. However, English has only five letters to represent these vowels: *a, e, i, o, u.* Obviously this is another challenge for learners: too many vowels; not enough letters. Additionally, many languages have only five vowel sounds. Therefore the total number of English vowels sounds and the insufficient number of vowel letters is a challenge.

The chart below shows the vowel sounds of English. Each vowel sound is represented by one or two letters that will be the symbols in this book for these vowel sounds.*

	front of mouth	central	back of mouth
high	EE ⟶ I	ER	OO ⟶ U
mid	AI ⟶ E	uh / UH	OY ⟶ O
low	A	AY ⟶ OU / AH	AW

The Key

Say each of these words.

Symbol	Sound		Symbol	Sound		Symbol	Sound
EE	beet		ER	Bert		OO	boot
I	bit		uh	<u>a</u>but		U	book
AI	bait		UH	ab<u>u</u>t			
E	bet		AY	bite		OY	boy
A	bat		AH	Bart		O	boat
			OU	bout		AW	bawl

*The phonetic alphabet used in this book is not one of the usual standards. (For a comparison with other common systems, see page 99-100 in the Appendix.) The system in this book was devised because it uses no "strange" letters (such as æ, ʃ, ə) or diacritic marks (˘ ~ ··), thereby imposing a second alphabet between the learner and the real English alphabet.

Now say a few more words for each of the sounds, write them below, and look at the spellings.

EE	AH
I	OU
AI	OO
E	U
A	OY
ER	O
UH	AW
AY	

Note: we will work on /uh/* later.

	AH	

	AH	

For worksheets, see page 40 in Section Two.

This is going to be easy. Relax! What sound do you make as you sit back and relax, perhaps with a cup of coffee or tea. Ahhhhhh! Or when you visit your doctor and the good doctor puts a tongue depressor on your tongue and says, "Open your mouth and say 'ah.'" Actually it's the only sound you can make easily with your tongue very flat and your mouth very open. Linguists call this vowel the low central vowel. Look at the chart. That's why /AH/ is placed in the low central spot on the chart. Actually, /AH/ is not a simple sound because, as we shall see, there are some variations among English speakers with the low central and low back vowels. But more on that later. For now, we're going to move our tongue and take on two very troublesome sounds.

*When we cite a sound, it will be written between slash marks.

EE and I

EE I		
	AH	

For worksheets, see pages 41 and 42 in Section Two.

If you say /AH/ with a tongue depressor on your tongue, and then move very quickly to say /EE/, as if you saw a cockroach run across your desk top, what happens? Try it.

You should feel your tongue moving up and forward in the mouth and at the same time, your mouth muscles tighten up, your mouth closes up a bit, and your lips and mouth will form a kind of grin. The /EE/ sound that you just formed is called the high front tense vowel. Now, if you relax your grin it will become the more relaxed /I/ as in "grin."

Try saying these pairs and phrases:

sit	seat	Sit in your seat.
bit	feet	It bit my feet.
still	steal	Is he still stealing?
Tim	team	Is Tim on the team?
Will	weak	Will's very weak.

These two sounds can be difficult for some learners because they have only one vowel in their language in this high front position, so they don't hear the difference easily, and consequently they can't make the difference easily. See page 43 in Part Two for an additional worksheet that addresses this problem.

Sit and *seat* is the first example of what we call a minimal pair. That means the only difference in these two words is the sounds /EE/ and /I/; in other words the difference in the two words is minimal because the /S/ and the /T/ sounds are an identical frame for the vowels. Look at the other pairs. Are they minimal pairs? (see Answers, p. 101)

At the end of this section is a technique called minimal pair practice that helps learners focus on a difficult sound and distinguish between two similar sounds.

And now let's move on to another pair of sounds, the mid-front vowels.

AI and E

EE		
I		
AI		
E		
	AH	

For worksheets, see pages 44 and 45 in Section Two.

Say this: *She stayed in bed.* If you compare the vowel in *stayed* with the vowel in *bed*, there is an obvious difference. What is it? Say these examples aloud. Look in the mirror as you say them carefully and deliberately:

fade	fed	hayed	head
raid	red	baste	best
fail	fell	take	tech

When you said an /AI/, did you notice your face starting to make a grin, and your mouth muscles begin to tighten up? That's because /AI/ is tense, like /EE/. And /E/ is relaxed, like /I/ (relaxed vowels are called "lax" vowels). You may also notice that /AI/ seems to be a longer sound, and it also seems almost like two sounds, /E/ and /EE/ said very rapidly together. This is something you could point out to a learner.

Although some learners may have difficulty discerning the difference between /AI/ and /E/, more learners will probably have difficulty with the difference between /I/ and /E/. Let's try some trios:

fin	fen	fade		wit	wet	wait
bid	bed	bade		pin	pen	paid
lid	led	laid		gin	Jen	jade
will	well	wail		wind	wend	wade
kin	ken	cane				

Would you agree that /I/ and /E/ would be more problematic? There is an additional worksheet on this problem on page 46 in Part Two.

And of course, as usual, there are spelling problems. In the trios above, what is one problem? Can you think of another common spelling for /AI/?
Check the Answers on page 101.

5

A		

EE		
I		
AI		
E		
A	AH	

For worksheets, see page 47 in Section Two.

The vowel /A/ has been made famous by "The Cat in the Hat." It is also the vowel sound with the most consistent one-to-one spelling: the letter "a." The sound itself is classified as low front. Say the vowels that we have covered so far: /EE, I, AI, E/and now /A/. Is /A/ tense or lax? Although it is the only low front vowel, it is often confused with /E/. For example, compare *man* and *men*. There is an additional worksheet on this pair on page 48 in Part Two. By the way, /A/ is lax.

Three-letter words with the vowel sound /A/:

cat   hat   pad   sap   _____   _____   _____   _____

_____   _____   _____   _____   _____   _____

Four-letter words with the vowel sound /A/:

flat   slat   grab   glad   _____   _____   _____   _____

_____   _____   _____   _____   _____   _____

ER

EE		ER	
	I		
AI			
	E		
	A	AH	

For worksheets, see page 49 in Section Two.

Many linguists would not consider this vowel to be a single sound, but describe it as a vowel plus consonant /R/. In fact it is almost a consonant. Say this: rrrrrrrrrrrrr. Is it a consonant sound or a vowel sound? For that matter, does it matter? The point is that for the learner, it is a unique sound that may have to be acquired. Secondly, it is a sound with six variant spellings: *er, ir, or, ear, ur,* and *ar*, as in *her, bird, word, heard, turn* and *liar.* Can you list some additional words with each spelling:

<u>er</u>   <u>ir</u>   <u>or</u>   <u>ear</u>   <u>ur</u>   <u>ar</u>

In some regions, the /R/ sound actually disappears so that the vowels in words like *word* and *bird* sound like "pure" vowels.

And it is a sound that is occasionally mispronounced by learners as /AR/or /EER/. For example, some learners may pronounce the word *bird* as /BARD/ or /BEERD/.

7

OO		

EE		ER	OO
	I		
AI			
	E		
		AH	
	A		

For worksheets, see page 50 in Section Two.

Say these words: *blue moon.* The vowel sound is the tense high back vowel. Notice that when you say this vowel sound your mouth tightens and your lips round. If you exaggerate it, even your throat muscles tighten. There are several spellings for this vowel sound. Add some more to the examples below.

oo	o...e	ue	ew	ui
moon	lose	blue	grew	fruit

And some unusual ones: *you, through, do, who, shoe,* to name a few. Notice what happened when you say *few.* The /OO/ sound is preceded by a /Y/ as in *you.* This is a variant that usually occurs when a word begins with /OO/. These words are often spelled with a "u": *unit, uniform, unique, universe, use,* etc. And there are a few other unusual spellings: *ewe, Europe.*

U

EE		ER		OO
	I		**U**	
AI				
	E			
	A	AH		

For worksheets, see page 51 in Section Two.

The companion to /OO/ is the short /U/ sound . It is also considered a high back vowel, but it is lax. It is the sound in *put* and *book.* In general, learners will have more difficulty with this sound and will tend to substitute a /OO/. It can also be confused with /OO/ because of the spelling, so that a learner may see *good* in print and pronounce it /GOOD/ rather than /GUD/. See a worksheet on this problem on page 52 in Part Two. Add some more examples to these two common spellings.

oo	u
book	put
_____	_____
_____	_____
_____	_____
_____	_____
_____	_____

Here are some unusual ones: could, should, would, w<u>o</u>man, wolf

9

UH

EE		ER		OO
	I		U	
AI		**UH**		
	E			
	A	AH		

For worksheets, see page 53 and 54 in Section Two.

The sound /UH/ is also the little word *uh* that we use as we talk to fill in a silence with a sound. It can even become irritating: "I will uh think about uh   what you uh have just said." When we are pausing or thinking and we don't want silence separating our words, out comes *uh*, neither high, low, front, nor back, just a nondescript mid-central vowel. Nevertheless, it is an important vowel in its own right when it is stressed. Some examples:

> but, cup, some, fun, one, ton, run, come, from, the, what, bum, shut

The spelling is messy, but the most common spelling is "u."

And /UH/ gets messier, as we shall see later on when we encounter stress in Section Two, because if a vowel does not get a lot of stress it tends to collapse to the mid-central position. The unstressed /UH/ is represented with /uh/. For now, to be a little more precise, we should say that /UH/ is the <u>stressed</u> mid-central vowel. We will look at the unstressed /uh/ on page 26.

Learners may confuse this vowel with others that are close to it physically. Which ones? Think about it as we move on to the next vowel.

AH and AW

EE		ER		OO
	I		U	
AI				
	E	UH		
	A	**AH**		**AW**

For worksheets, see pages 40 and 55 in Section Two.

And here we are, back to our vowel of relaxation, the low central vowel. And yes, it is sometimes confused with /UH/. Say the two. There isn't much difference, is there? So look for a minimal pair practice on page 54 in Part Two. And while you're at it, /UH/ and /U/ can be confusing, as in *buck* and *book*.

As mentioned before, there is a problem in this area of the vowel system. In a word like *father* the first vowel is clearly a pure low central vowel. Another example is *calm*, although there may a slight difference in the two vowels in *father* and *calm* because of the following consonant that tends to have some influence on the vowel sound (this happens a lot). In fact, /AH/ is often followed by /R/, as in *hard* or *car*, and we can say that the /AH /is "colored" by the /R/. In some parts of North America, the /R/ is dropped, as in the well-known, "*I parked my car in Harvard yard.*" (PAHKT, CAH, HAHVuhD, YAHD)

The second complication is that for many speakers, the vowel in the word *not* is very similar to the vowel sounds in *father* and *calm*. In fact we can consider them the same vowel because they are all part of the same phoneme. However, some speakers will use a different sound for the "not" words – for short words with the letter "o," as in *cop, dog, hot, got*, etc., they may use /AW/ as in *ball*. Arrange the words below in two lists, /AH/ and /AW/, according to how YOU say them.

Park, moss, far, spot, heart, cross, talk, shot, haul, flaw, palm, yard, bottle, shop, taught, claw, all, pot, harm, stop, mall, cot, froth, pasta, lawn, log, cough, frost, par, crop, caught, call, flop, straw

AH   AW

11

AY

EE		ER		OO
	I		U	
AI		UH		
	E			
	AY			
A		AH		AW

For worksheets, see page 56 in Section Two.

This vowel can be considered to be two vowels blending together (called a diphthong). /AY/ begins with /AH/ and moves very quickly to /EE/. For example, you touch something hot and say *Ay Ay Ay*! Notice how the sound glides from /AH/to /EE/. This sound is not a huge pronunciation problem for most learners.

There are some spelling considerations. First note the use of *y* as in *my, by, try, fly*. Second, another common spelling is the letter *i* followed by the "silent e", as in *side, file, smile, time, nice*. And then there is the strange spelling "igh" as in *sigh, fight, slight,* and *night*.

OU

EE		ER		OO
	I		U	
AI		UH		
	E			
	AY	**OU**		
A		AH		AW

For worksheets, see page 57 in Section Two.

This is what you say when you stub your toe or hit your head. Like /AY/, it begins as an /AH/ and then moves toward an /OO/ as in, *Ow!* or *Ouch!* This is not usually a problem sound for learners, although it may be a new sound. The spelling can be troublesome. Like the symbol OU for the sound, there is the spelling *ou* as in *out, bout, pout*.

However, many words follow the "how now, brown cow" spelling of /ow/.

O and OY

EE		ER		OO
	I		U	
AI			**OY**	**O**
	E	UH		
		AY	OU	
	A	AH		AW

For worksheets, see pages 58 and 59 in Section Two.

We are using only one letter to represent the sound /O/, which is the sound in *go* and *show*. However, the English "o" is really a glided sound that starts with /O/ but ends up almost as /OO/. And that is reflected in the spelling of many /O/ words: *throw, blow, crow.*

This sound should not be a major problem for most learners, although they may make a "purer" /O/ without the /O + OO/.

The sound /OY/ is also a glided sound like /AI/ and /AY/. It starts out as an /O/ and ends up as an /EE/. The spelling is always *oy* or *oi.* For fun, you can introduce these sounds with the phrase, "*Oh, boy!*"

13

The Consonants

The chart below shows the 24 English consonants:

Labial/Labio-dental	Dental	Alveolar	Palatal	Velar
P B		T D		K G
F V	th TH	S Z	CH J SH ZH	H
M		N		NG
W		L R		Y

The Key

Say each of these words.

Symbol	Sound
P	pay
B	bay
T	tie
D	die
K	kill
G	gill

Symbol	Sound
F	fan
V	van
th	thigh
TH	thy
S	sue
Z	zoo
CH	cheap
J	Jeep
SH	asher
ZH	azure
H	hash

Symbol	Sound
M	sum
N	sun
NG	sung
L	lice
R	rice
W	wield
Y	yield

Consonant Articulation

The vowels are made as air comes up from the lungs, passes through the vocal cords, and reverberates in the mouth as the tongue and lips change the shape of the mouth. Consonants are more complicated, and to understand them we first have to take a look at the parts of the mouth. Some parts are very obvious, so let's start there. #1 lips – also known as the labia, #2 teeth – also known as dentals, #3 tongue,* #4 alveolar ridge – that hard ridge just behind the teeth, #5 palate – the roof of the mouth, #6 velum – the soft, back part of the roof, #7 the nasal cavity, #8 the vocal cords.

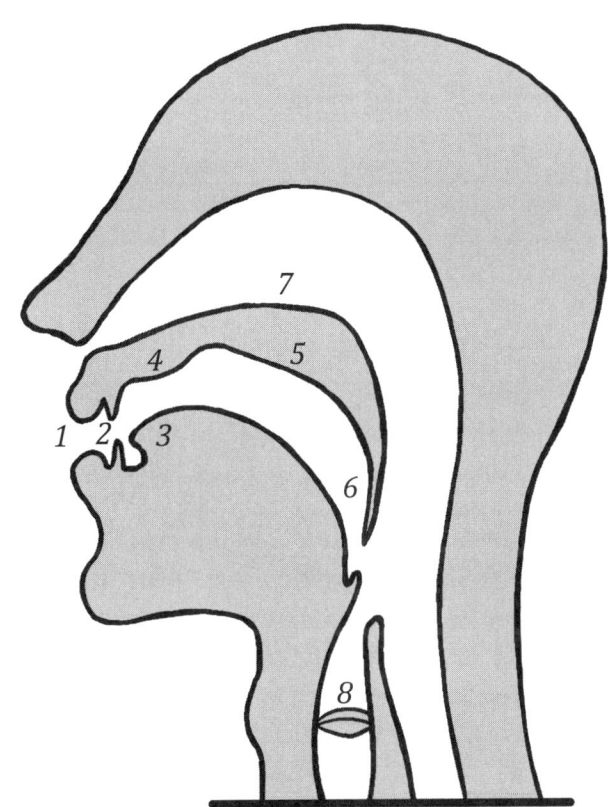

#1 lips
#2 teeth
#3 tongue
#4 alveolar ridge
#5 palate
#6 velum
#7 the nasal cavity
#8 the vocal cords.

In addition to the place where consonants are shaped, there is another important feature we need to explain before we jump into the middle of the consonants. It is voicing. Many of the consonants come in pairs, for example /P/ and /B/. Say *pat's bat*. What is the biggest difference in these two consonants? They are both produced in the same place in the mouth – at the lips – and they are both said with a puff of air, although /P/ is a stronger puff. To put it simply /P/ is quiet and /B/ is noisy. What that means is that as a /B/ is formed, the air coming up from below causes the vocal cords to vibrate and produce sound. When /P/ is said, the vocal cords do not vibrate. There is no sound, i.e. /P/ is voiceless and /B/ is voiced.

> * Have you ever noticed how languages often use the word *tongue* to mean language?
> English: *Mother tongue*, French: *langue*, Spanish: *lengua*, Turkish: *dil.*

The stops:
P and B   T and D   K and G

Labial/Labio-dental	Dental	Alveolar	Palatal	Velar
P B		T D		K G
F V	th TH	S Z	CH J SH ZH	H
M		N		NG
W		L R		Y

P and B   *For worksheets, see page 60 in Part Two.*

The sounds /P/ and /B/ are very similar in the way they are formed. Air coming from the lungs is stopped momentarily by the two lips and then released. The result is a puff of air, especially with /P/. An old trick for demonstrating this is to hold a lighted match (or a thin piece of paper) just in front of the mouth. A /P/ will blow the match out. The /B/ will not. This puff of air is called aspiration. Many languages do not aspirate the voiceless stop /P/, and so their /P/ may sound more like a /B/, and some languages do not have a /P/ and so in asking for a pear they would say *bear* instead of *pear*. You may need to work on this.

T and D   *For worksheets, see page 61 and 62 in Part Two.*

/T/ and /D/ behave much like /P/ and /B/, that is /T/ is voiceless and aspirated, where-as /D/ is voiced and not aspirated. /T/ can blow out a match, /D/ does not. There is another difference with English /T/s and /D/s. Say *top* and notice where your tongue is. Your tongue touches the alveolar ridge, whereas in many languages these sounds are made with the tongue touching the teeth, not the alveolar ridge. This is not a serious problem because it will usually not result in misunderstanding, but if accent improvement is the goal of the teaching, this could be something to work on.

K and G *For worksheets, see page 64 in Part Two.*

And the final pair of stops, /K/ and /G/, are again a voiceless and voiced pair. For these two sounds, the air is stopped and released in the back of the mouth at the velum. There is much less aspiration with the /K/. Usually there is not a serious pronunciation problem here, but there are some spelling problems.

How is the sound /K/ spelled? The answer: <u>k</u>ey, <u>c</u>ap, ba<u>ck</u>, <u>ch</u>orus, and as part of qu as in <u>q</u>uick.

What about /G/? No problem here, except for the doubling, as in egg, and bigger.

Special Note on the Pronunciation of "-ed"

The regular past tense ending in English is spelled with "ed," and " ied" if the verb ends in a "y." But there are three pronunciations of the "ed."

If the verb ends with a voiceless consonant sound (P, K, F, S, SH, or CH), the pronunciation is simply /T/ as in,
  talk > /TAWKT/, *tap* > /TAPT/, *kiss* > /KIST/.

If the verb ends with a voiced consonant sound (B, D, G V, Z, TH, J, M, N, NG, L, R, W, or Y), the pronunciation is /D/ as in,
  hug > /HUHGD/, *hum* > /HUHMD/, *buzz* > /BUHZD/

If the verb ends with a vowel sound (vowels are voiced), the pronunciation is /D/ as in,
  free > /FREED/, *cry* >/KRAYD/, *flow* > /FLOD/

And if the verb ends with /T/ or /D/, a syllable is added, as in *wait* > /WEYTID/, *add* > /ADID/.

There is an additional worksheet on this problem on page 63.

17

The Fricatives

Labial/Labio-dental		Dental		Alveolar		Palatal		Velar	
P	B			T	D			K	G
F	**V**	**th**	**TH**	**S**	**Z**	**CH** **SH**	**J** **ZH**	**H**	
M				N				NG	
W				L	R			Y	

The next group of eleven consonants is called fricatives because they all are formed by forcing the air through a narrow channel which causes friction and a kind of hissing sound. Again we will see that most of these sounds have voiceless and voiced pairs.

S and Z *For worksheets, see page 65 in Part Two.*

To begin, let's look at a voiceless /S/ and a voiced /Z/. Start out with a hiss, like a snake, /S/, and then switch to a /Z/ like a snore. Note that the lips are open but the teeth remain closed, and as a result the air is constricted and vibrates as it passes by the alveolar ridge and the teeth. Some learners will substitute the /S/ for the /Z/. So you may need to do some work here. One spelling problem here is that some /Z/ sounds are spelled with "s," as in *as*, and *is*. And there are some /S/ sounds that are spelled with a "c," as in *city*.

The "-s" ending on Verbs and Nouns

The "s" that is used for plurals (*dogs*), third person singular verbs (*hugs*), and possessive "s," (*Bill's*) is spelled "s," "es," or "ies" (for words ending in "y"), but there are three pronunciations.

> If the word ends in a voiceless sound, the "s" is pronounced /S/ as in *walk* > /WAWKS/, *lip* > /LIPS/.

> If the word ends in a voiced sound, the pronunciation is /Z/ as in *beg* > /BEGZ/, *bed* > /BEDZ/, *Bill's* > /BILZ/.

> If the word ends in /S/, /Z/, /SH/, /ZH/, /CH/, or /J/, a syllable is added, as in *bus* > /BUHSIZ/, *buzz* > /BUHZIZ/, *wish* > /WISHIZ/, *itch* > /ICHIZ/ *edge* > /EJIZ/.

There is a worksheet on this problem on page 66 in Part Two.

F and V *For worksheets, see page 67 in Part Two.*

This pair is made when the upper teeth rest on the lower lip and the air passes between the teeth and lip. There may be some problems here when learners use /F/ in place of /V/, for example, /OFER/ for /OVER/. However, a more common problem is probably the confusion between /V/ and /B/, as in *berry* instead of *very, or bowel* instead of *vowel.*

th and TH *For worksheets, see page 68 in Part Two.*

The next pair represents a problem for many learners because many languages do not have these sounds. They are similar in the way they are made, with the tongue actually slightly between or up against the teeth. The tongue rests on the lower teeth, and the sound escapes between the top of the tongue and the teeth. And again we have a voice-less /th/ and a voiced /TH/. Although they can be confused for each other, the more common problem is substituting stop consonants or fricatives. For example, /th/ as in *think* is pronounced as "tink" by some learners and "sink" by others. And /TH/ as in *that* is pronounced as "dat" or "zat." See the additional worksheets on pages 69 and 70.

The only spelling for these sounds is "th."

SH and ZH *For worksheets, see page 71 and 72 in Part Two.*

These are the sounds in *show* and *pleasure.* The first voiceless sound is fairly common in English, but the second one, the voiced /ZH/, is not very common. As such it is not a big pronunciation problem. /SH/, however, does present some problems because it is simi-lar to /CH/, which we will look at shortly. As for spelling, the /SH/ sound is frequently spelled "sh," although it may be spelled "s" as in *sure*, and in the strange combination of "ti" or "ss" as in *attention* or *mission* and other "-tion" and "-sion" words.

List a few words that have the /SH/ sound and the spellings below:

<u>sh</u>   <u>ss</u>   <u>ti</u>

19

CH and J *For worksheets, see page 71 in Part Two.*

These two sounds are called affricates. They are a combination of a stop and a fricative. If you sneeze ("a-a-a-choo!") you are making an affricate. The air builds up, but is prevented from escaping (a stop) and then it is released, and it becomes a fricative.

As mentioned earlier /CH/ is often confused with /SH/ and may need some work.

Spelling: "ch" is the most common and reliable spelling for the /CH/ sound, although sometimes it will be spelled "tch." As for /J/, the most common spelling is "j" although sometimes "g" is used, as in *George,* or "dg" as in *judge.*

ZH and SH *For worksheets, see page 72 in Part Two.*

As mentioned before, /ZH/ is not a common sound in English. Learners may substitute /SH/ for it. The spelling is usually with a "g," as in *beige, garage,* and *mirage,* or with an "s" followed with a "u," as in *pleasure.*

H *For worksheets, see page 73 in Part Two.*

/H/ is the only non-paired fricative. And the friction is created throughout the entire oral cavity beginning at the velum. This sound is not really a problem, although there are words that are spelled with an initial "h" that do not have any sound: *honor,* and some words like *although* and *high* that have a soundless "gh."

It should also be noted that some speakers of English pronounce the "wh" words as if they were /HW/, for example /HWUHT, HWEYR, HWEN, HWAY, while other speakers do not do this. For them, these "wh" words are pronounced /WUHT, WEYR, WEN, WAY/.

The Nasals: M, N, and NG

Labial/Labio-dental	Dental	Alveolar	Palatal	Velar
P **B**		T D		K G
F V	th TH	S Z	CH J SH ZH	H
M		**N**		**NG**
W		L R		Y

For worksheets, see page 74 in Part Two.

These three sounds are all voiced sounds made primarily in the nose.

/M/ is made when the mouth is closed and the air comes up from the throat and reverberates in the nasal cavity. It's the sound we make when we hum. When an /N/ is made, the sound is stopped by the tongue blocking the sound at the alveolar ridge, causing the sound to go into the nose; the /NG/ sound is made when the sound is blocked at the velum and goes into the nose. Of the three sounds, the /NG/ can be troublesome. Learners will sometimes see a word such as *sting* and pronounce it as /NG + G/, so that it will sound like /STING-GA/. And note the irregular spelling of *tongue*.

The Liquids: L and R

Labial/Labio-dental		Dental		Alveolar		Palatal		Velar	
P	B			T	D			K	G
	F V	th	TH	S	Z	CH SH	J ZH	H	
M				N				NG	
W				**L**	**R**			Y	

For worksheets, see page 75 in Part Two.

/L/ and /R/ are problem sounds. In the first place, many learners have difficulty making the North American /R/. It is not tapped, flapped, or trilled as it is in many languages. As mentioned in the section on vowels, it is almost like a vowel. Although the tongue is involved, the tongue does not touch anything; it curls back and holds that curled back position as the sound goes over and around it.

The /L/ is formed somewhat like the /R/ because the tongue forms a position in the mouth, but with this sound it curls up slightly and actually touches the alveolar ridge. The sound coming up from the vocal cords slides around but not over the tongue. Speakers of many languages have difficulty in forming and hearing these two sounds and will need to practice them.

Like its cousin /R/, /L/ can act like a vowel as the final sound of a word. Say *total*. Is it /TOTuhL/, two syllables, or /TOTL/ with the /T/ and /L/ fusing together? This can happen with several final consonants. Say and listen to these words.

apple	awful	puzzle
total	oval	channel
puddle	missile	

The only spelling problem is the silent "l" in words like "Linco_l_n" and "ca_l_m." Can you find a few more?

22

Glides: W and Y

Labial/Labio-dental		Dental		Alveolar		Palatal		Velar	
P	B			T	D			K	G
	F V	th	TH	S	Z	CH SH	J ZH		H
M					N				NG
W				L	R			**Y**	

For worksheets, see pages 76 and 77 in Part Two.

The last two consonants can also fulfill a vowel-like role.

Say *Wow*! The first "w" is like a consonant. It precedes the vowel and it starts almost as if it were going to be /OO/, but it never becomes /OO/. It is followed immediately by a vowel: *we , win, way, wet, were, won, wan, woo, wool, woe, war.* As you will see if you look in a mirror, the main physical feature is a rounding of the lips. And notice how the final sound in *wow* is a perceptible /OO/ and the lips are rounded as they are with the first /W/. In a sense, the final sound is half vowel and half consonant. Some learners have a problem saying /W/ and may substitute a /V/ or a fricative sound similar to /V/.

As noted before in the description of /H/, some speakers of English pronounce most "wh" words as if they were /HW/, for example /HWEN/, while other speakers do not do this. For them, *When* is pronounced /WEN/, not /HWEN/.

/Y/, like /W/, exhibits this same characteristic of performing both as a consonant and as a vowel. Say "Yay!" as your team scores a goal. We start to say /EE/, but after shaping the mouth, another vowel may come out: *yip, yet, Yale, yap, yup, yikes, yard, yaw, young, you, yo.* The letter "y" at the end of a word, as in *say, fly,* and *boy,* is actually representing the glide vowels /AI/, /AY/, and /OY/. This sound is usually not a big pronunciation problem, nor is it a significant spelling problem.

Consonant Clusters

For worksheets, see page 78 in Part Two.

English has a large number of two-letter and three-letter consonant clusters, as in <u>black</u>. <u>br</u>ow<u>n</u>, <u>gr</u>een, ora<u>nge</u>, <u>str</u>ipe, <u>spl</u>ash, <u>spr</u>i<u>ng</u>. However, not all consonant clusters have more than one sound. Among the words above, *ck in bla<u>ck</u>* and *ng* in *spri<u>ng</u>* are single sounds. The pronunciation problem occurs when two or three consonant sounds have no vowel between them. Learners may try to insert a vowel. This problem is especially true of learners whose languages do not have many clusters but are more regularly consonantvowel-consonant-vowel-consonant–vowel, etc., in words such as *hippopotamus* > HIP uh PAHT uh MUHS > CVC V CVC V CVC.

Clusters can occur initially, medially, and finally. There are almost 50 possible initial clusters of two or three sounds. Many of these can be found medially, especially after prefixes, for example, *sleep > asleep*. However, English has as many as 170 final clusters. Obviously, it would be too time consuming to try and address every single potential mispronounced cluster. Nevertheless, there are several common initial consonant clusters that begin with "s" and are problematic for many learners. They tend to put a short vowel just before the "s," resulting in pronunciations such as ESPANISH (*Spanish*) ESKOOL (*school*), uhSMOK (*smoke*), ISTRAHNG (*strong*).

The handout on page 78 provides examples of the most common initial clusters. In the space below, collect a few medial and final clusters. By the way, there are a few final clusters with four letters (but not always four sounds). Can you think of any?
See page 101.

The Suprasegmental Phonology System

As the term suggests, this aspect of phonology deals with the aspect of sound and pronunciation that overlays the individual segments of sound. At its basic level it affects loudness of syllables (stress) and the pitch of syllables (intonation).

As syllables are strung together in flowing speech, vowel reduction and linking take place, and the utterances result in rhythmic phrasing.

Syllabification

For worksheets, see page 79 in Part Two.

Before taking on the first element of the suprasegmental system, it is worthwhile to review the concept of "syllable." Simply put, a syllable is a unit of sound that has a vowel at its core and possible consonants before and after the vowel. A syllable can be simply a single vowel sound (V), for example the *a* in *pro nun ci a tion,* or a consonant and vowel (CV), as in *ci,* or CCV as in *pro,* or CVC as in *nun* and *tion.* The following are common English syllable patterns.

V	C-V	C-V-C	C-C-V-C	C-C-C-V-C	C-C-C-V-C-C
/EE/	/TEE/	/TEEM/	/STEEL/	/STREEK/	/STRENGth/

In multisyllable words it is not always easy to tell where one syllable ends and another begins, so when in doubt consult a dictionary. The main point is that there must be one and only one vowel in every syllable. As we shall see in the next section, stress will fall on that vowel. Break each word in this list into syllables and show the syllable pattern. The first one is done.

_____ review	re view	CV CCV
_____ column		
_____ headline		
_____ newspaper		
_____ editorial		
_____ opinion		
_____ classified		
_____ political		
_____ accident		
_____ international		
_____ information		
_____ advertisement		

Answers on page 101.

Stress

For worksheets, see page 81 in Part Two.

Stress in linguistic terms refers to the amount of energy that a syllable receives when it is uttered. In simpler terms, it is how loud the syllable is. A stressed syllable is louder and usually a bit longer than the other syllables in a word or phrase.

Primary Stress

Remember that a syllable includes one vowel sound with one or more consonant sounds before and/or after the vowel, although a syllable can be just a vowel sound. Say the words below, break them into syllables, and underline the loudest syllable.

Example: Canada   <u>Can</u> a da

Boston	Minneapolis
Cleveland	Philadelphia
Ontario	Los Angeles
Nebraska	

Answers on page 101.

Weak Stress

Now let's take a closer look at two-syllable words in English and observe the stress. Say these words and underline the stressed syllable, for example, <u>Port</u>land.

listen   pencil   vowel   common   purpose   English

If you say these words at normal speed, do you notice that the vowel in the second syllable is very weak, even hard to hear?

● .   ● .   ● .   ● .   ● .   ● .
LIS uhN   PEN suhL   VOU uhL   CAHM uhn   PER PuhS   ING LuhSH

Weak stress is even more common in multisyllable words. Underline the weak stresses in these words.

constitution   declaration   amendment   capitalism   representative   congressional
Check the Answers on page 101.

THIS IS A VERY IMPORTANT FEATURE OF SPOKEN ENGLISH.

Because stressed syllables consume so much energy (long and loud), the syllables that are not stressed lose energy, and their vowels tend to lose their identity and collapse to the mid-central area inhabited by unstressed /uh/. In fact, the unstressed /uh/ has a special name: schwa – a very nondescript sound that is barely audible. In this book we use /uh/ to indicate this sound and call the stress "weak." Also note that for learners, it can be challenging to develop their listening comprehension skill because so much of what they hear is unstressed and barely audible. *For worksheets, see page 84 in Part Two.*

Secondary Stress

For worksheets, see pages 82 and 83 in Part Two.

Now say these words. Underline the primary stress and notice the second syllable.

Pronoun   notebook   laptop   phoneme   email   keyboard

In this series of words something different happens. Let's look at *pronoun*. The "*pro*" is stressed, right? But the "*noun*" is too, agreed? *Noun* is not as loud as *pro*, but it is still loud enough for us to hear the quality of /OU/ in noun. What we have here is secondary stress.

We will therefore consider English to have three levels of stress: primary (●), secondary (●), and weak (•).

Compound Word Stress

You may also have noticed that in the second group of words, there are actually two words joined together to form a new word. This process is called compounding, and most compound nouns follow the stress pattern of primary-secondary.

● •   ● •   ● •   ● •   ● •   ● •
PRONOUN   NOTBUK   LAPTAHP   FONEEM   EEMAIL   KEEBORD

Although this stress pattern is common for nouns, many compound verbs (including phrasal verbs), and adjectives often have the reverse pattern:

● • ●   • ●   • ●   • ● •   • ● •
overcome   log on   look up (a word)   far-reaching   outstanding

A final note on two-syllable words (It actually applies to multi-syllable words as well), some of them have the stress on the second syllable. However, there are many more two-syllable words that stress the first syllable. Check this out with any written passage. What percentage are stressed on the second syllable?

Here are a few:

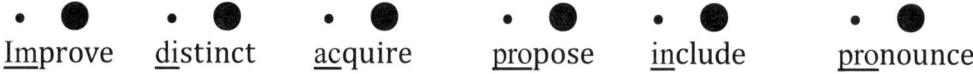

Im<u>prove</u>   <u>dis</u>tinct   <u>ac</u>quire   <u>pro</u>pose   <u>in</u>clude   <u>pro</u>nounce

Notice that these words have a prefix (underlined, above). This is a common pattern in English. If a word has a prefix , the prefix does not get much stress.

Stress on Multisyllable Words

For worksheets, see page 82 and 83 in Part Two.

Take a look at this word: *Pronunciation.* Say it normally.

> How many syllables?
> Which syllable gets the heaviest (primary) stress?
> Which syllable gets some (secondary) stress?
> What happens to the stress on *pro ci   tion?*
> What happens to the vowels in *pro* and *tion?*

As previously mentioned, the stress system has an effect on the vowels. If they are not stressed, they tend to become schwa. But notice that *ci* still maintains some of its full vowel sound of /EE/. Nevertheless, listen to how the syllables /NUHN/ and /AI/ dominate the word. We could make a case for tertiary stress, but for our purposes, the terms "primary," "secondary," and "weak" are sufficient, keeping in mind that there is "weak" and "weaker."

Here are a few more words to mark for primary and secondary stress.

Individual	complicated	problematic	suprasegmental
Nevertheless	secondary	interpretation	intonation

Answers on page 101.

This distribution of stress on words and phrases will have an effect on the intonation and rhythm of spoken English. We will investigate this further on.

Sentence Stress

For worksheets, see page 85 in Part Two.

In addition to stress acting on words at the word level, stress also affects an entire sentence. Say this: *Maria's friend is from Mexico.* Which syllables are stressed?

You probably chose *ri*, *friend,* and *Mex* for heavy stress, and *co* for secondary stress. However, *Mex* has the heaviest stress of all. This is the normal stress pattern in a declarative sentence. The last primary stress gets the heaviest stress – "super primary." It signals that the end of the sentence has been reached, and something new is about to happen – another sentence or a response from a listener. We'll use ● for "super primary" stress.

Emphatic Stress

For worksheets, see page 86 in Part Two.

As indicated above, there is a "normal" stress pattern to a declarative sentence. However, in the give-and-take of normal conversation, speakers often use stress to call attention to specific parts of a sentence. For example, look at these questions and answers.

Who is that?
That's Maria's FRIEND.

Where is she from?
She's from MEXICO.

Whose friend is that?
That's MARIA'S friend.

Who is from Mexico?
Maria's FRIEND is from Mexico.

Intonation

For worksheets, see pages 87, 88, and 89 in Part Two.

Intonation is all about the melody of the language; its ups and downs from low notes to high notes. In general, it works with stress so that stressed syllables are not only louder, they have a higher tone. The most significant part of the intonation of a sentence is the final tone. Say this sentence as a statement of fact:

The daffodils are in bloom on Welcome Hill.

A normal statement finds the voice dropping at the end of the statement.

The daffodils are in bloom on Welcome Hill.

Now make it a question:

Are the daffodils in bloom on Welcome Hill?

And now begin your sentence, but don't complete it because you want to say something else.

The daffodils are in bloom on Welcome Hill, and

So we have three intonation contours: Statement, Yes/No question, and Incompletion.

There are three other patterns to note. First, an information (WH) question:

How are the daffodils on Welcome Hill?

Usually the intonation falls at the end of an information question. If a question word is used for the purpose of clarification, the sentence will end on rising intonation.

I didn't understand.
How are the daffodils on Welcome Hill?

When a series of words or short phrases are spoken, notice the rise and fall of the intonation.

The daffodils, violets, and pansies are in bloom.

And when there is an alternative:

Either the daffodils or the pansies are in bloom.

30

Linking

For worksheets, see pages 91 and 92 in Part Two.

When words are spoken as part of a phrase, it is very common for words to fuse together, as if they were one word. One common pattern is when a word ends with a consonant sound it will link up with the following word if it begins with a vowel sound. For example:

green apple	*red onion*	*black olive*	*navel orange*
GREENAPL	REDUHNYuhN	BLAKAHLIV	NAIVuhLARuhNJ

Another common pattern is that, if a word ends in a glided vowel sound (EE, AI, AY, OU,or OO), it will link up with the following word if that word begins with a vowel sound. For example:

three years	*day after*	*dry up*	*how often*	*too easy*
thREEYEERZ	DAIAFTER	DRAYUHP	HOUWAWFuhN	TOOWEEZEE

For the same reason, we have *a* and *an,* two phonological variants that perform this task (*a book* and *an apple*). The /N/ of *an* joins with the following vowel sound so that *an apple* becomes /uhNAPL/. For a similar reason, consider *the.*

The book > /THuhBUK/ The apple > /THEEAPL/

So, consider this sentence: *I bought an apple, an orange, and an onion.* Try writing it out in phonemic script. In regular script it would be: I bought anapple, anorange andanon-ion – this latter phrase said as if it were one long word.

Answers on page 102.

Phrasing
(Also called "Thought Groups")

For worksheets, see pages 93 and 94 in Part Two.

It should be obvious that in the flow of normal conversation, a lot is happening: individual sounds, stress, intonation, and linking. But that's not all. As English flows along from utterance to utterance there are subtle pauses and a rhythm to the flow of sounds. The pauses are often correlated with the comma, semicolon, colon, and period of written English. But pauses often correlate with grammatical phrases in a sentence, so that in a sentence such as: *My good friend Jack has a house in downtown Minneapolis,* the words clump together into grammatical phrases.

<u>MygoodfriendJack</u>	<u>hasahousein</u>	downtown<u>Minneapolis</u>
Noun phrase	verb phrase	adverbial (prepositional phrase)

Of course, this is a tendency, not a hard and fast rule. Speech is too complicated to be easily analyzed into rigidly fixed patterns. In fact, in the sentence above, the *in* is grammatically part of the prepositional phrase, but the tendency to link overrides grammar and pulls *house* and *in* together. Try grouping these sentences:

The pronunciation of English can be difficult.

The spelling system doesn't reflect the sound system adequately.

Many of the sounds are spelled with several different letters.

With practice your students will be able to speak well.

We have seen how in individual words, some syllables with their vowels lose their stress, and the vowel tends to collapse to a weak mid-central position /uh/. We have also seen how the stressed syllables predominate in sentences, and usually there is one syllable that stands out as having "super primary" sentence stress. But let's take a look at what happens to the unstressed syllables in a sentence. Look at this sentence:

This is an example of a sentence that in the spoken language isn't simply a string of unconnected words.

First read it with a momentary pause between each word and the next.

This..is..an..example..of..a..sentence..that..in..the.. spoken..language..isn't..simply..a ..string.. of.. unconnected..words.

In actual speech it would sound like this:

> Thisisanexample..ofasentence..
> thatinthespokenlanguage..isn'tsimply..astringof..
> unconnected..words.

To be sure, different people might read the sentence in slightly different ways, but virtually everybody would tend to utter groups of words as if they were single words. Now, if we were to collapse the unstressed syllables it would sound like this:

> This_{isan}exam_{ple}.._{ofa}sen_{tence}.._{thatinthe}spok_{en}lan_{guage}.._{isn't}simply..
> _astring_{of}..un_{con}nect_{ed}..words.

The result is we have ten stressed syllables and seventeen unstressed syllables, and the unstressed vowels in the sentence have collapsed toward the mid central schwa. AND for the listener, these unstressed syllables are very hard to hear – a real listening comprehension challenge. In fact, listeners will depend on their knowledge of the lexicon and grammar to supply the almost-missing sounds. In the above sentence, "this" is loud and clear and the listener expects it to be the subject of the sentence followed by a partially heard word "example." If the listener is familiar with the word "example" they will hear the full word and quite probably connect "this" and "example" with the copula "be" followed by the article "an" that can precede a noun.

Listening comprehension is not the subject of this book on pronunciation, but practicing saying strings of words with stress and reduction can benefit listening comprehension.

Rhythm

For worksheets, see page 95 in Part Two.

To conclude this exploration of the suprasegmental system, there is one more aspect to consider: the natural rhythm of spoken English.

Say these verb phrases and note the rhythmic pattern:

they teach

they have taught

they have been teaching

they will have been teaching

The progression of syllables in the phrases above goes from two to six, and yet all four phrases can be said in about the same amount of time, because we instinctively collapse the unstressed syllables. English poetry, especially rhymed poetry, shows this tendency very clearly. Look at the rhythmic pattern of a simple limerick.

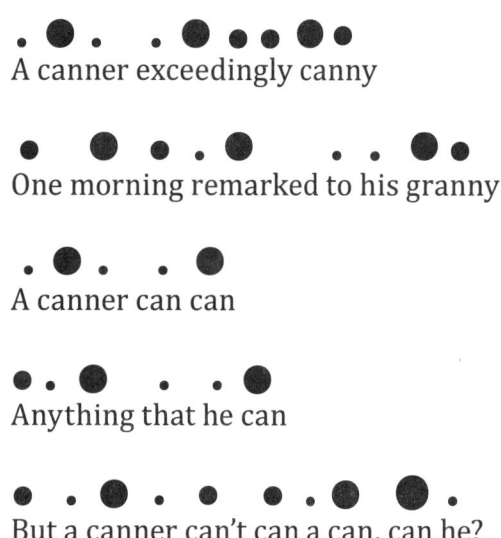

A canner exceedingly canny

One morning remarked to his granny

A canner can can

Anything that he can

But a canner can't can a can, can he?

The limerick has a basic rhythmic pattern that characterizes this type of short poem. And the distinguishing feature of the poem is the number of stressed syllables in each line: 3-3-2-2-3.

And take a look at one more example from poetry, where Longfellow has established a pattern of four stressed syllables per line.

The Paul Revere statue at Old North Church, Boston

Listen my children, and you shall hear
Of the midnight ride of Paul Revere,
On the eighteenth of April in Seventy-five;
Hardly a man is now alive
Who remembers that famous day and year.

He said to his friend, "If the British march
By land or sea from the town tonight,
Hang a lantern aloft in the belfry arch
Of the North Church tower as a signal light, –
One if by land, and two if by sea;
And I on the opposite shore will be,
Ready to ride and spread the alarm
Through every Middlesex village and farm,
For the country folk to be up and to arm."

English speech, whether poetic or not, is marked by a rhythm called stress-timed rhythm. This is in contrast to many other languages where the rhythm is called syllable-timed rhythm, in which each syllable is more or less the same length as the preceding and following syllables, in contrast to English's alternation of stressed and unstressed (weak) syllables.

Teaching Pronunciation

Simply put, there are two approaches to teaching pronunciation:
planned and unplanned.

Planned means preparing a lesson focusing on some aspect of pronunciation, and like the classical form of a lesson plan, there is usually a **presentation** of the point in question, **practice** of the point, in which the learner engages in a structured, controlled activity, and finally, **production** or **use** of the point, in which the learner is using the point of the lesson more or less freely. Unplanned teaching is when a student's attempt to communicte is hindered by poor pronunciation, and the teacher steps in with a model or correction. Let's take a brief look at these approaches one at a time.

Planned Teaching

First of all, even planned teaching of pronunciation is not usually done without some reference to an event or situation that has created a need for the lesson. In other words, a pronunciation problem has occurred, perhaps one that the learners may remember. For example, in the middle of a conversation class a student from Pakistan is telling about his village in Swat. He has just talked about having a picnic near a river. Another student asks, "Do you keep sheep there?" and he responds, "Oh, we have only small sheeps to use on the river." The teacher notes this problem with /I/ and /EE/ and decides to do some work on that tomorrow (sooner is better than later) because other students are having the same problem (in fact this /EE~I/ problem is almost universal).

So, the teacher plans a minimal pair practice, introducing it to the class with, "What's the difference between a ship and a sheep?" In other words, the origin of the planned practice is a perceived problem, and the students may recognize the reason for practicing the /I~EE/ distinction. In Part Two there are several handouts that can be used for planned pronunciation lessons: minimal pair practice, stress placement practice, intonation practice, and chants or poems for working on all of the above, along with rhythm.

Doing a minimal pair drill should not take long, and as the handouts show, is best accompanied with other brief activities where the key sounds are placed in the context of phrases and sentences.

Minimal Pair Drill Procedure

One way to do the practice is to number the pairs, Sound 1 and Sound 2, as below:

1	2
bit	beat
did	deed
fill	feel
hip	heap

Note that single-syllable words work best.

1. Begin by saying the words in column 1 as the students listen.

2. Then say the words in column 2 as the students listen.

3. Then say the words across: "bit, beat,"* as the students continue to listen.

4. You say words randomly, asking the students to say "one" or "two" or hold up one or two fingers.

5. Then have the students repeat after you chorally

   a. down column 1

   b. down column 2

   c. across the columns

6. Then point and have students say the words chorally

   a. down

   b. across

   c. in random order

7. Point for individuals to respond.

*try to keep your intonation the same on both words: *bit, beat,* not *bit, beat.*

Unplanned Teaching

This type of teaching really works best with a phoneme problem ("heat" instead of "hit") or with a problem of misplacing stress (pro BLEM, instead of PRO blem).

Obviously it is not good practice to stop at every mispronunciation, so the first consideration has to be: "Is this worth a brief interruption" in a lesson which may be conversation or grammar practice? That is, of course, a judgment call, but one overriding concern should be: does the problem interfere with communication? Another consideration is: is this a problem for many of my students?

Having decided the problem warrants immediate attention, what do we do?

1. You step in and try to fix the problem.
                or
2. You make a note and attend to it later.

The advantage to the "quick fix" is of course that it is immediate feedback. The disadvantage is that it interrupts something else, and the student's focus is not necessarily on your correction. Hence, nothing may change. In fact, developing accurate pronunciation is not something that usually happens with only one or two "corrections." It takes time to change habitual behavior.

There are many variations on the "quick fix" practice, in addition to simply saying the word correctly for the student. One is to have already done a planned lesson of some kind in which key words such as *beat* and *bit* illustrate the problem. So the student says, "He heat me," and you say, "Is that 'heat' or 'hit?'"

A wall chart displaying the phonemes is very useful. A quick point or tap at the chart without your saying anything can be effective because the student is not merely parroting what you say, but trying to recall and reformulate on their own, i.e. self-correcting.

The best approach is probably a combination of the two approaches.

Part Two
Photocopyable Worksheet Handouts

***The Handouts on the following pages are mostly self-explanatory,
but a few notes may be helpful.***

Working with Vowels and Consonants.

The vowels are introduced one at a time. Many of the consonants are introduced in pairs, usually to compare and contrast similar sounds. The handouts include these activities.

Listen and Say: You may want to precede this with a description of how the sound is made. Then the learners simply say the words after you.

Phrases: The featured sounds are practiced within a phrase for listening and saying. Do both group and individual responses.

Sentences: Try to use sentence-level stress and intonation, as well as the featured sounds.

Rhymes (vowel work only): Encourage the learners to find and list rhyming words.

For Fun: Also work on the rhythm.

Pair Practice: Refer to the Minimal Pair procedure on page 37.

Working with the Suprasegmental System.

The basic procedure is to model the words, phrases, and sentences, with the learners repeating. Alternatively, instead of saying the words, "da-da" the syllables, calling attention to the stress, intonation, and rhythm can also be useful.

Using the CDs.

An advantage to using the CDs is to have two more voices so the learners can listen to natural variations in speech. Using the CDs also lets you pay close attention to what the learners are saying without thinking about what you need to say next.

AH

Vowels

	AH	

Listen and Say

o	a	others
box	father	guard
shop	want	heart
clock	star	ought
top	calm	
doctor	Harvard	

Phrases

a box of chocolates   not a lot of rocks
a lot of pots   not a lot of knots
a flock of swans   not a lot of locks
a talking clock   lots and lots of blocks

Sentences

The job in the shop was hot.
The top of the box was locked.
The yacht at the dock was stopped.
The swan's song was long.

Rhymes

block	spot	fox	star
_____	_____	_____	_____
_____	_____	_____	_____
_____	_____	_____	_____

For Fun

A charming young doctor from Guam
Observed, "The Pacific's so calm,
     I'll swim for a lark!"
     He met a large shark –
Let us now sing the ninetieth psalm.

CD 1 ✳ **Track 2**　　　　　　　　**EE**

Vowels	**EE**		
		AH	

Listen and Say

ee	ea	e..e/ea..e	others
meet	meat	Pete	police
feel	clean	theme	machine
free	heat	eve	seize
green	sea	ease	receive
cheese	leaf	grease	brief
tree	weak	weave	he

Phrases

a green tree	a greedy thief	an easy team to beat
a deep stream	a sleepy priest	a greasy piece of meat
a clean sheep	a piece of cheese	a green and leafy tree

Sentences

He can eat the meat.　　　　　She can keep the key.
She can feed the sheep.　　　　Edith can heat the tea.
We can meet the queen.　　　　Peter can clean the street.
She needs a week of sleep.　　　The sea is green and deep.
The teacher needs a key.　　　　Did you see the scene with Caesar?

Rhymes

feet	cheap	seem	she
_____	_____	_____	_____
_____	_____	_____	_____
_____	_____	_____	_____

For Fun　　Marie had a serious dream
While asleep by a very deep stream.
　　　　The dream seemed so real
　　　　She thought she could feel
At her knee in the sea a green seal.

I — CD 1 ✳ Track 3

Vowels

EE		
I		
	AH	

Listen and Say

i	**y**	**others**
big	myth	busy
trick	hymn	build
wish	syllable	women
swim	symbol	pretty

Phrases

a big ship   a thin pin
a thick stick   a sick pig
a rich kid   a quick trip

Sentences

The dish is in the kitchen.   Mrs. Smith is sick.
The kids are in the picture.   Mr. Bliss is rich.
The chicken's in the window.   Billy Kidd is big.
The kid in the kitchen is Billy.   The prince and the princess are busy.
The ship in the river is sinking.   The pig is kissing the kitten.

Rhymes

fish   gym   lip   skin

_____   _____   _____   _____

_____   _____   _____   _____

_____   _____   _____   _____

For Fun

This little pig went to market,
This little pig stayed home,
This little pig had roast beef,
This little pig had none.
And this little pig cried, "wee-wee-wee-wee-wee,"
All the way home.

42

| **CD 1 ✳ Track 4** | **Pair Practice 1:** | **EE ~ I** |

Vowels

1	2
beat	bit
leave	live
sheep	ship
reach	rich
seat	sit
easy	is he

Sentences

She hid the key.	The cliff is steep.
We missed a week.	The pig is clean.
He kicked the sheep.	The river's deep.
The thief hid the key in the kitchen.	The priest didn't swim in the river.
The dish in the kitchen is greasy.	The queen and the princess are busy.

For Fun

Scissors and string, scissors and string;
When a man's single he lives like a king.
Needles and pins, needles and pins;
When a man's married, his trouble begins.

A silly young man named Bill Beebee
Was in love with a lady named Phoebe.
    "But," said he, "I must see
    What the marriage fee be
Before Phoebe be Phoebe B. Beebee.

AI

Vowels

EE		
I		
AI		
	AH	

Listen and Say

a..e	ai	ay	others
game	sail	day	break
take	paid	say	great
change	rain	play	eight
gave	main	way	weight
save	wait	hay	they

Phrases

a great day	a rainy day	a pale stain	a great day in May
a late plane	a lazy maid	an aching pain	a painted gate
a brave face	a famous name	a gray gate	fair play

Sentences

Ladies hate to wait.
Paint the table gray.
Take the tray away.
Bake the cake today.

The rain delayed the game.
We play at eight today.
The gate was painted gray.
The ape will break the cage.

Rhymes

ace	pain	take	flame
_____	_____	_____	_____
_____	_____	_____	_____
_____	_____	_____	_____
_____	_____	_____	_____
_____	_____	_____	_____

Proverbs and Idioms for Fun

An apple a day keeps the doctor away.
Rome wasn't built in a day.
Better safe than sorry.
All work and no play makes Jack a dull boy.

Make hay while the sun shines.
Save it for a rainy day.
Hit the nail on the head.

CD 1 ✳ Track 6		E

Vowels

EE			
	I		
AI			
	E		
		AH	

Listen and Say

e	ea	others
bed	bread	friend
when	wealth	said
dress	breath	any
egg	meant	guest
bet	sweat	

Phrases

the red dress
the deaf friend
the dead pet
the best pen

the healthy men
the western friend
the wealthy guest
the friendly pet

Sentences

The red hen was dead.
The dress was wet.
The guest was deaf.
The bet was ten cents.

The flesh on his neck was red.
The hen's eggs were fresh.
The rest of the bread was wet.
The men's friends were dead.

Rhymes

west   head   cent   spell

_____   _____   _____   _____

_____   _____   _____   _____

_____   _____   _____   _____

_____   _____   _____   _____

For Fun

A young English teacher named Pell
Was teaching his students to spell.
    No student would dare
    Confuse their, there, and they're
Or else he would send them to hell.

Pair Practice 2: I ~ E CD 1 * Track 7

Vowels

1	2
lift	left
listen	lesson
did	dead
fill	fell
if	F
bigger	beggar
wrist	rest

Sentences

She couldn't find her pin.	He played with ten soldiers.
She couldn't find her pen.	He played with tin soldiers.
She slept on the street.	He bit twenty cents.
She slipped on the street.	He bet twenty cents.
He sent her a scent.	She sent him a cent.

For Fun   Did Peter Bickle pick a peck of pickled peppers?

A peck of pickled peppers? Which peck of peppers?

A peck of pickled peppers in a paper bag.

A little bag of pickled peppers

Or a big bag of pickled peppers?

The bag of pickled peppers, beside the little bed.

But the bag beside the little bed has no peppers;

It's a bag of Peter Bickle's papers,

And Peter couldn't pick pickled peppers.

Peppers are pickled only after they're picked.

CD 1 ✳ Track 8	A		

Vowels	EE		
	I		
	AI		
	E		
	A		
		AH	

Listen and Say

<u>a</u>
add
back
chance
grand
tax

Phrases

a bad map   as a matter of fact
a sad fact   an animal act
a black bag   a basket of cats
a fat rat   a valley of rats

Sentences

The captain had a cat.   The actor laughed at Jack.
The back of the cat is black.   Dad was mad at the brat.
That rat is fat and black.   The animal act was last.
The cat on the mat was sad.   Pat sat on a fat black bat.

Rhymes

cat   glass   dance   crack   crab

_____   _____   _____   _____   _____

_____   _____   _____   _____   _____

_____   _____   _____   _____   _____

_____   _____   _____   _____   _____

For Fun   Jill gave Jack a new backpack,
              And they climbed the hill together.
              But Jack fell flat and whacked his back
              So Jill took Jack's backpack back.

47

Pair Practice 3: A ~ E ~ I CD 1 ✳ Track 9

Vowels

1	2	3
laughed	left	lift
batter	better	bitter
tan	ten	tin
dad	dead	did
pack	peck	pick
bat	bet	bit
bag	beg	big

Sentences

He saw the men.
He saw the man.

He's going to send it.
He's going to sand it.

She couldn't find her pen.
She couldn't find her pin.
She couldn't find her pan.

For Fun

Two men from the Isle of Man
Decided to get a nice tan.
　　One man got red,
　　And the other one said,
"I'll get redder than that if I can."

A handsome young master named West,
Gave his class quite a difficult test.
　　He failed all those who
　　Confused to, too, and two,
But happily passed all the rest.

CD 1 * Track 10　　　　　　　　**ER**

Vowels	EE		**ER**	
		I		
	AI			
		E		
		A		
			AH	

Listen and Say

er	ir	or	ur	ear
nerd	bird	word	fur	heard
verb	third	work	hurt	earth
herd	sir	worse	Turk	earn
Serb	stir	world	curl	

Phrases

hurt at work	curly fur	a third of the world
Turks and Serbs	the first verb	the worm turned
clerk of the works	worse than murder	an absurd nerd
a whirly bird	third degree burns	perfect for surfing

Sentences

His words hurt Herb.　　　　　We heard a whirly bird.
His fur was burned.　　　　　His work is getting worse.
Who heard the bird?　　　　　The turtle was hurt.
What is the worst place on Earth?　His shirt is dirty.

Rhymes

bird　　　　　fur　　　　　turn　　　　　girl　　　　　clerk

_____　_____　_____　_____　_____

_____　_____　_____　_____　_____

_____　_____　_____　_____　_____

_____　_____　_____　_____　_____

For Fun　　There once was a poet from Turkey
　　　　　　Whose poems were absurd and quite quirky.
　　　　　　　　He used many words
　　　　　　　　But rarely used verbs.
　　　　　　So the lines in his verse herky jerky were.

OO

Vowels

EE		ER		OO
	I			
AI				
	E			
	A			
		AH		

Listen and Say

oo	u..e	ew	ue	others	
boot	rude	new	blue	fruit	who
moon	rule	grew	true	suit	two
cool	dude	threw	glue	through	
tool	mule	blew	flue	do	

Phrases

a loose tooth   a spoonful of soup
a blue suit   a beautiful suit
a cool room   a youth group

Sentences

Who moved the fruit?   Prove that the rule is true.
Who knew the truth?   Move to a cooler room.
Who threw the shoe?   Susan fools around in school.

Rhymes

choose   shoe   truth   soon   school

_____   _____   _____   _____   _____

_____   _____   _____   _____   _____

_____   _____   _____   _____   _____

_____   _____   _____   _____   _____

For Fun

A tutor who tooted a flute
Tried to tutor two tooters to toot.
    Said the two to the tutor,
    "Is it harder to toot, or
To tutor two tooters to toot?

CD 1 ✳ Track 12　　　　　　　**U**

Vowels	EE			OO
		I		**U**
	AI			
		E		
	A			
			AH	

Listen and Say

oo	u	ou	others
book	put	would	woman
wood	bush	could	wolf
good	pull	should	
wool			

Phrases

a good book　　　　　　good wood
a good cook　　　　　　a good cookbook
a crooked crook　　　　push and pull
by hook or by crook　　look and put

Sentences

A crook took the book.　　　　　　　It was good, but I'm full.
Look for the cook.　　　　　　　　　I would if I could.
He works with wood.　　　　　　　　He took a look at Brooke.
The woman put her foot in the brook.　The cook wouldn't look for the book.

Rhymes

book　　　　would　　　　pull

_____　_____　_____

_____　_____　_____

_____　_____　_____

_____　_____　_____

For Fun

How much wood could a woodchuck chuck
If a woodchuck could chuck wood?
If a woodchuck could chuck wood,
A woodchuck would chuck
As much as he could chuck,
If a wood chuck could chuck wood.

Pair Practice 4: OO ~ U CD 1 * Track 13

Vowels

1	2
pool	pull
stewed	stood
Luke	look
wooed	wood
fool	full
shooed	should

Sentences

The food is good.
The pool is full.
The book is blue.

The bull is loose.
The view is good.
The suit is wool.

Who cooked the good food?
Who took the blue wool?
Who used the woolen suit?
Who glued the wooden stool?

Poem for Fun

A woolly old bear at the zoo
Could always find something to do.
　　When it bored him to go
　　On a walk to and fro
He reversed it and walked fro and to.

Proverbs and Idioms for Fun

It's too good to be true.
Now the shoe's on the other foot.
No news is good news.
What's good for the goose is good for the gander.
Too many cooks spoil the broth.
If the shoe fits, wear it.

52

CD 1 * Track 14   # UH

Vowels	EE			OO
		I		U
	AI			
		E	**UH**	
	A			
			AH	

Listen and Say

u	o	ou	others
but	son	young	none
luck	from	touch	some
rug	month	rough	come
shut	of	tough	flood
thud	ton	en<u>ou</u>gh	blood

Phrases

under the rug   above the sun   in front of the hut
under the gun   above the cup   in front of the gun
under her thumb   a lucky duck   the front of the drum

Sentences

Some of the money was under the rug.
One of the brothers was sucking his thumb.
None of his sons touched his gun.
He sold honey and bunnies and made tons of money.

Rhymes

sun   thumb   funny   was

_____   _____   _____   _____

_____   _____   _____   _____

_____   _____   _____   _____

_____   _____   _____   _____

For Fun   Fuzzy Wuzzy was a bear,
                Fuzzy Wuzzy had no hair.
                Fuzzy Wuzzy wasn't really fuzzy,
                was he?

53

Pair Practice 5: H ~ AH CD 1 ✳ Track 15

Vowels

1	2
come	calm
bud	bard
hum	harm
fund	fond
stuck	stock
rubber	robber

Phrases

hot cross buns	a box of bugs
a lucky shot	a two-ton hog
a muddy yard	a hard-hearted thug
a shuttered shop	hundreds of frogs

Sentences

We lugged the logs to the hut.	The clock struck one.
The bus won't stop for us.	Tons of rocks struck the bus.
What's in the stockpot?	The rock made him stumble.
What nut tied this knot?	

For Fun

Hickory dickory dock,
The mouse ran up the clock.
The clock struck one
and down he did run.
Hickory dickory dock.

54

CD 1 ✳ Track 16	AW

Vowels			
EE			OO
	I		U
AI			
	E	UH	
	A		
		AH	**AW**

Listen and Say

aw	**al**	**au**	**o**
law	all	cause	cloth
draw	ball	fault	cross
raw	fall	pause	long
saw	talk	haul	soft

Phrases

salty sauce	a ball in the hall	a strong law
a soft cloth	a long haul	because it's wrong
Paul's dog	a small loft	all the loggers

Sentences

He saw a small dog.   There's a flaw in the law.
He called it a ball.   Let's overhaul the law.
Paul paused in the hall.   Is there salt in the sauce?

Rhymes

law	tall	cross	dog	talk
_____	_____	_____	_____	_____
_____	_____	_____	_____	_____
_____	_____	_____	_____	_____
_____	_____	_____	_____	_____

For Fun   Hot cross buns!
Hot cross buns!
One a penny, two a penny,
Hot cross buns!
If you have no daughters,
If you have no daughters,
If you have no daughters,
Give them to your sons.

55

AY

Vowels	EE			OO
	I		U	
	AI			
	E	UH		
	A	**AY**		
		AH	AW	

Listen and Say

i..e	y	i	igh	others
bite	by	bind	tight	tie
five	sky	I	might	dye
life	dry	mild	sight	eye
time	my	kind	fight	buy

Phrases

a wild ride	a fine drive	a dry fly
a bright light	a white wine	a nice price
a mild night	a white pine	a high rise

Sentences

Why does he cry at night?   Try to arrive on time.

Mice are a frightening sight.   White mice like rice.

She cried at the sight of the mice. Why did it die?

He tried to be kind to the child.   The time was right.

Rhymes

sign	white	my	rice	ride
_____	_____	_____	_____	_____
_____	_____	_____	_____	_____
_____	_____	_____	_____	_____
_____	_____	_____	_____	_____

For Fun

As I was going to St. Ives,
I met a man with seven wives;
Each wife had seven sacks,
Each sack had seven cats,
Each cat had seven kits,
Kits, cats, sacks, and wives,
How many were going to St. Ives?

CD 1 ✳ Track 18	OU

Vowels

EE		ER		OO
	I		U	
AI				
	E	UH		
A		AY	**OU**	
		AH		AW

Listen and Say

ou	ow
cloud	ow
south	brown
out	now
house	town
flour	flower

Phrases

a brown cow	about the house
a loud sound	without a doubt
a proud scout	around the town
down on the ground	a pound and an ounce

Sentences

The clown fell down.	The sound in the town was loud.
The mouse was brown.	The brow of the cow was brown.
The cow was found.	The shout from the crowd was loud.

Rhymes

town   out   around

_____   _____   _____

_____   _____   _____

_____   _____   _____

For Fun   Downtown Brown has a brown hound
That hangs around the town; it thinks it's a clown.
It makes no sound; it just lounges around
In the park on the ground.
The cops came around, put the hound in the pound.
It cost Brown a pound to get his brown hound
Out of the pound.

57

O

Vowels	EE		ER			OO
		I			U	
	AI		uh			**O**
		E	UH			
		A	AY	OU		
			AH		AW	

Listen and Say

o	oa	o..e	ow
go	coat	rose	row
no	boat	home	know
so	load	those	blow
roll	toad	smoke	crow

Phrases

an old coat	over the hole	a rolling stone
a slow boat	over the road	a frozen nose
a cold stove	over the phone	a broken bone

Sentences

The goat in the road was old.
The stone in the hole was gold.
The snow on the slope was cold.
Let's go! Get the show on the road!

Rhymes

those	own	grow	hole	road
_____	_____	_____	_____	_____
_____	_____	_____	_____	_____
_____	_____	_____	_____	_____
_____	_____	_____	_____	_____

For Fun: A Re-done Round

Row, row, row your boat
Floating down the flow.
Slowly, slowly, slowly, slowly,
Going with the flow.

CD 1 ✳ Track 20	OY

Vowels

EE		ER			OO
	I		U		
AI		uh	**OY**		O
	E	UH			
	A	AY	OU		
		AH		AW	

Listen and Say

oy	oi
toy	toil
boy	boil
joy	join
annoy	voice

Phrases

a noisy toy	joyful noises
a loyal boy	joyful voices
an oily toy	noisy voices
the royal soil	annoying noises

Sentences

Roy, please oil your noisy toy.   The boys enjoyed the toys.
He was boiled in royal oil.   Were the noisy boys nosy?
What noise annoys an oyster?   Noisy boys annoy an oyster.
Joy and Roy do not enjoy soy.

Rhymes

toy   oil

_____   _____   _____   _____

_____   _____   _____   _____

_____   _____   _____   _____

For Fun   "Your tiller needs oil," said Roy to the toiler.
"Its noise annoys as you till the soil."
Said the toiler to Roy, "my dear boy,
I do not enjoy your nosy ploys.
Go soak your nose in oil and soy.
I'll till this soil without using oil."

59

| P and B | | | | | | CD 2 ✳ Track 1 | |

Consonants

P B			T D		K G
F V	th TH	S Z	CH J / SH ZH	H	
M		N		NG	
W		L R		Y	

Listen and Say

1	2
pet	bet
pan	ban
Pete	beat
Paul	ball
pin	bin

Listen and Say

lip	lop	lope	tap	bap	pap	pup	stop	slop	cup
lib	lob	lobe	tab	bab	pab	pub	stab	slab	cub

open	apple	ripple	paper	popper	rapper
obey	rabble	rubble	robber	rubber	bobby

Phrases

my pet lab	play ball in the pool	a rapid rabbit
a sub in the pub	a boat in the bay	a baby bug
baking paper	an improper robber	ripples on the pond

Sentences

Pat plays baseball with Paul's bat.
A bad apple spoils the barrel.
A bundle of paper was put on the porch.
Peter picked up a baseball bat and proceeded to pummel the potatoes.
The people at the party bobbed for apples and pears.

60

CD 2 ✳ Track 2			T and D					

P B		**T**	**D**		K G
F V	th TH	S	Z	CH J / SH ZH	H
M		N			NG
W		L	R		Y

Consonants

Listen and Say

1	2
too	do
tell	dell
teal	deal
tip	dip
tam	dam
tamper	damper

Listen and Say

let	bet	vet	wet	set	get	fret	met	state	great
led	bed	ved	wed	said	ged	Fred	med	stayed	grade

wetter	waited	water	better	butter
wedder	waded	wadder	bedder	budder

Phrases

tell a tale	deep in debt	a better bed
take a break	down in the dumps	a dead duck
a two-dollar bill		

Sentences

Ted let his two teddy bears eat dinner in the dining room.
Don saw Tom dive in the tiny but deep duck pond.
Della drove downtown for tea and a dozen tasty doughnuts.
Fred said he'd get good grades and attend Denver Tech.
"Wait!" Donna told Dick, "Don't taste the meat!"
Twenty two-dollar bills is not twenty-two dollars, dummy!

Consonants

Pair Practice: T and D   **CD 2** ✳ **Track 3**

1	2
town	down
eight	aid
too	do
tide	died
bet	bed
plate	played
train	drain

Phrases

take a test	a dear daughter	a tragic day
try a taste	a dull dinner	a dirty train
tell a tale	a dangerous desert	a tiny dish
turn on the TV	a dark day	a terrific dentist

Sentences

Take the tickets to the teacher.   Her daughter didn't die.
Tell the teacher to be tactful.   The doctor doesn't drive.
Take a taxi to the temple.   The donkey didn't drown.

For Fun

An unhappy lad from New Trent
Decided to live in a tent.
    He dug a ditch round it
    But pretty soon found it
Better to rent in Old Trent, so he went.

62

Consonants

| CD 2 ✻ Track 4 | Regular Past Tense "-ed" |

Listen to the final sound of these words that end in "ed."
     wiped, walked, laughed, missed, wished, watched
What is the final sound?

Now listen to these words.
     Rubbed, hugged, saved, bathed, buzzed, raged, named, signed, called, cared
What is the final sound?

Now listen to these words.
     freed, played, rowed, cried
What is the final sound?

Now listen to these words.
     waited, wanted, rented, needed, ended, graded
What is the final sound?

To form the regular past tense:

1. Words that end with the sounds P, K, F, S, SH, CH, add the T sound. These sounds are called voiceless.
2. Words that end with B, G, V, TH, Z, J, M, N, NG, L, R add the D sound. These sounds are called voiced.
3. Words that end with a vowel sound like EE, AI, O, AY add the D sound.
4. Words that end with a T or D add ID.

Practice

In pairs take turns answering your friend's question. Use the word "thingamajig."
For example: What did you need ? I needed a thingamajig.

1. What did you inspect?	9. What did you want?
2. What did you like?	10. What did you push?
3. What did you smell?	11. What did you try?
4. What did you paint?	12. What did you trade?
5. What did you notice?	13. What did you pull?
6. What did you enjoy?	14. What did you carry?
7. What did you touch?	15. What did you close?
8. What did you open?	16. What did you use?

K and G

Consonants

P	B			T	D			K	G
	F V	th	TH	S	Z	CH J SH ZH		H	
	M			N				NG	
	W			L	R			Y	

Listen and Say

1	**2**
kit	git
cap	gap
kill	gill
ache	egg
bake	beg

Listen and Say

Ken	cat	call	pick	tack	backer	cuff	cash
gen	gat	gall	pig	tag	bagger	guff	gash

backpack	piggyback	backtrack	plastic bag
grab bag	gray dog	kickback	Hackensack

Phrases

guys and gals	a gaggle of geese	King Kong
a bag of candy	a gallon of Coca Cola	good as gold
a pig in a poke		

Sentences

He kicked a goal.
The gray goose is gone.
The kitten caught a bug.
Kim baked a cake.

For Fun

An unhappy young gal from Kentucky,
Who was always extremely unlucky,
    Set out in her car
    To go very far,
But got stuck 'cause the road was quite mucky.

Consonants

| CD 2 ✳ Track 6 | | | | | S and Z | | | | |

P	B			T	D			K	G
	F V	th	TH	**S**	**Z**	CH J SH ZH		H	
	M			N				NG	
	W			L	R			Y	

Listen and Say

	1	**2**
	price	prize
	race	raise
	Sue	zoo
	place	plays
	loose	lose
	close	close

Phrases

a slow start	a safe speed	a soft song
safe and sound	a loose tooth	nice rice
lazy girls	crazy boys	busy bees
the zebra at the zoo	a dozen daisies	frogs' legs
a crazy place	a priceless prize	the city zoo

Sentences

He received a prize for first place in the race.
Sally likes to sew dresses.   The bees were busy and buzzing.
She hopes to pass science.   The boys were crazy and dizzy.
Sally wants to see Sammy.   The bears were Fuzzy and Wuzzy.

For Fun

In the Gambia, a Zambian musician
Playing jazz made a fateful decision.
   He picked up the bongo
   And went to the Congo
Where now he's a famous physician.

Simple Simon met a pieman going to the fair;
Said Simple Simon to the pieman, "Let me
   taste your ware."
Said the pieman to Simple Simon, "Show me
   first your penny."
Said Simple Simon to the pieman, "Sir, I
   haven't any!"

Consonants

The "-s" Ending   CD 2 ✳ Track 7

Listen to the final sound of these plural nouns and verbs that end in "s."
> **Nouns:** cups, cats, ducks, graphs, moths
> **Verbs:** taps, hits, knocks, buffs

What is the final sound?

Now listen to these words.
> **Nouns:** labs, words, eggs, caves, rooms, sons, songs, camels, bears
> **Verbs:** rubs, holds, begs, raves, seems, runs, sings, pulls, fears

What is the final sound?

Now listen to these words.
> **Nouns:** horses, mazes, dishes, watches, ridges, garages
> **Verbs:** crosses, raises, wishes, catches,

What is the final sound?

To form the "S" endings:

Words that end with the sounds P, T, K, F, th: add the S sound. These sounds are called voiceless.

Words that end with B, D, G, V, M, N, NG, L, R: add the Z sound. These sounds are called voiced.

Words that end with S, Z, CH, SH, J, or ZH: add IZ.

Practice

Pronounce the following pairs of words.

coats and codes	cups and cubs	elf's and elves	tacks and tags
kits and kids	caps and cabs	cats and cads	rips and ribs
locks and logs	pats and pads	wife's and wives	picks and pigs

Use a noun plural in this question: *Where are the _____?*

map	cuff	pencil	scratch	bowl	pad
glass	number	wing	tongue	paper	badge
hat	bug	basket	forest	cake	spoon
edge	watch	pen	robe	apple	lesson
room	frog	rose	island	song	slave
church	ladder	cave	name	dish	bridge

Ask and answer. *What does a taxi driver do? He drives a taxi.*

horse trader	song composer	tax collector	drug pusher
apple picker	duck hunter	lion tamer	bank robber
window decorator	dress designer	tourist guide	fire fighter
dish washer	sign painter	math teacher	mail carrier

                 Photocopyable for classroom use.

Consonants

CD 2 ✳ Track 8			\$	F and V				
P	B			T	D		K	G
	F **V**	th	TH	S	Z	CH J	H	
						SH ZH		
M				N			NG	
W				L	R		Y	

Listen and Say

1	2
fan	van
feel	veal
fine	vine
leaf	leave
life	live
rifle	rival
few	view

Listen and Say

face	far	fat	fair	life	loaf	laugh	tough	cough
vote	veer	vat	vain	love	dive	Dover	never	river

avoid	invade	develop	overdrive	volleyball
affect	afraid	differ	effective	effervescent

Phrases

over and over	a fanatic fan	few and far between
the love of his life	fast and furious	the White Cliffs of Dover
a vast valley	a very beautiful view	forever and ever

Sentences

She lived a very active life, and she believed in "Live and let live."
The vampire bat flew fast and far to find his victim.
Fred Flintstone flies fancy kites from his cave.
Very few voters voted for the vice-president.
It's a very fine wine from a very fine vine.

Consonants

th and TH

CD 2 ✳ **Track 9**

P B		T D		K G
F V	**th TH**	S Z	CH J SH ZH	H
M		N		NG
W		L R		Y

Listen and Say   th

thin	think	thought	both	tooth	mouth
path	myth	faith	thumb	thank	earth
throw	death	breath	bath	cloth	

Listen and Say   TH

the	this	that	these	those
thy	mother	father	brother	either
neither	breathe	bathe	clothe	

Phrases

through thick and thin	all thumbs	once a month
a stone's throw	a bed and bath	thread and a thimble

this and that	that was then	these and those
here and there	fathers and sons	either this or that

Sentences

I have a toothache, a sore throat, and a dry mouth.
Both his brothers thanked his father for thinking about taking them to
    the theater.
That's the path through the woods that I think we need to take.
The thin old man breathed his last breath, and Death took him away.
Whatever the weather, whether nice or not, if we think nice thoughts,
    everything will be all right.

Consonants

CD 2 ✳ Track 10 Pair Practice: T and th

1	2
tin	thin
true	threw
team	theme
debt	death
bat	bath
boat	both

Phrases

take a test	both of the threads
tell a tale	both of the thoughts
take a trip	both of the thorns

two of the faiths	two of the myths
two of the deaths	two of the cloths

Sentences

Tom tasted the tea.	The thin youth was thoughtful.
Tim talked to the team.	The three thieves were thirsty.
Ted took off his tie.	The south path was thorny.

We thought the test was on Thursday.
I thanked the teacher for trying.
She took her theme to the teacher.

For Fun
The north wind doth blow, we soon shall have snow,
And what will poor robin do then? Poor thing!
He'll sit in the barn to keep himself warm,
And hide his head under his wing. Poor thing!

For Fun
Rub-a-dub-dub, three men in a tub.
And who do you think they be?
The butcher, the baker, the candlestick maker,
And all of them gone to sea.

Consonants

Pair Practice: D and TH CD 2 ✳ Track 11

1	2
day	they
dare	there
den	then
ladder	lather
udder	other
load	loathe

Phrases

dancing in the dark	The other brothers
digging in the dirt	the other mothers
dreaming in the day	the other fathers
another dollar	during the other day
another dinner	during the other dance
another daughter	during the other drama

Sentences

Didn't they bathe there?	Didn't they breathe that?
Didn't they clothe them?	Don't wear leather in this weather.
Don't dress in those clothes.	Don't bother your dear brother.

For Fun

Yankee Doodle went to town
a-riding on a pony.
Stuck a feather in his cap
and called it macaroni.

Chorus
Yankee Doodle, keep it up,
Yankee Doodle dandy.
Mind the music and the step,
And with the girls be handy.

Father and I went down to camp
Along with Captain Gooding;
And there we saw the men and boys
As thick as hasty pudding.

(chorus)

Consonants

CD 2 ✳ Track 12			SH, CH, and J				
P B			T D			K G	
	F V	th TH	S Z	**CH** **J**	H		
				SH ZH			
M			N			NG	
W			L R			Y	

Listen and Say

1	**2**	**3**
sheep	cheap	jeep
shock	chalk	jock
shill	chill	Jill
ship	chip	jip (gyp)
bash	batch	badge

Phrases

edge	ledge	lodge	badge	large	bridge	budge	bulge	jury
edger	ledger	lodger	badger	larger	bridger	judge	indulge	July

a cheap jeep   a cheap shot   a chip shot

shipshape   a watched pot   The Red Badge of Courage

Sentences

Roger watched Chip's sheep chew his shoe.

The jeep bashed in the Dodge's door, jumped the ditch, and hit the ledge.

Jack washed his shirts and socks at the seashore with cheap soap, and they shrank.

Jim brought a large jug of orange juice just for us.

Which witch wished for a jet for the journey to Jamaica?

For Fun   A shepherdess from marshy Manchuria,
Who was known as a terrible worrier,
Watched over her sheep
In a bright orange jeep
For fear they'd run off with a furrier.

Consonants

ZH and SH

CD 2 ✳ **Track 13**

P B		T D		K G
F V	th TH	S Z	CH J **SH ZH**	H
M		N		NG
W		L R		Y

Listen and Say   ZH

beige	barrage	mirage	garage	azure	occasion
pleasure	treasure	measure	leisure	seizure	rouge

it's a pleasure   Treasure Island   a desert mirage   at your leisure

by any measure   a serious seizure   beige is the rage   a barrage of words

Listen and Say   SH

mesh	assure	passion
masher	pressure	special
trash	mission	official

Sentences

It's a pleasure to meet you.
The treasure was found in the garage.
She bought a beige and azure leisure suit.
The barrage hit the garage.
Who used my rouge?
Did she choose the red rouge?
It's a special occasion.
The mission was accomplished.
The officials reached closure on the trash issue.

72

Consonants

| CD 2 ✻ Track 14 | | | H | | | | |

P B			T	D			K G
	F V	th	TH	S	Z	CH J	H
						SH ZH	
M				N			NG
W			L	R			Y

HW

what, when, where, why, which wheel, whether, while, whip, whisper, white
Where is the great white whale? When and where will we see it?

H

who, whose, whole
hem and haw   his and hers   hard headed   hit or miss   here and there
hell or high water   hither and yon   house and home   hard of hearing

Ø

honest, honor, hour

a happy hour   an honest cop   an honor roll

For Fun   A greedy old hoodlum named Harry
        Stole more than he really could carry.
            With hardly room in his sack
            Nor in his backpack,
    In the garden the loot Harry buried.

Vowel review

he	heard	who
him	hub	hood
hay	hoist	hold
head	hide	how
had	hard	hall

Consonants

M, N, and NG				CD 2 ✳ Track 15
P B		T D		K G
F V	th TH	S Z	CH J / SH ZH	H
M		**N**		**NG**
W		L R		Y

Listen and Say

M	**N**	**NG**	
Some ham	sun hand	sung hang	
hum dim	Hun din	hung ding	
rum	run	rung	

NG	**NGK**	**NG**	**NGG**
thing sting	think stink	singer stinger	finger linger
sing bang	sink bank	hanger banger	hunger anger

Phrases

sing a song   sing along   the morning sun
ding dong   a stinking skunk   the skunk stank
a skating rink   a fingernail   a singer of songs
a tingling tongue   a ring finger   rum did dee dum

Songs

Ding, dong, bell,
Pussy's in the well.
Who put her in?
Little Johnny Thin.
Who pulled her out?
Little Tommy Stout.
What a naughty boy was that,
To try to drown poor pussy cat,
Who never did him any harm,
But killed the mice in the farmer's barn.

Sing a song of sixpence,
A pocket full of rye,
Four and twenty blackbirds
Baked in a pie;
When the pie was opened,
The birds began to sing,
Wasn't that a dainty dish
To set before the king?

| CD 2 ✳ Track 16 | | | L and R | | | |

Consonants

P B			T D		K G
F V	th TH	S Z	CH J / SH ZH		H
M		N			NG
W		**L R**			Y

Listen and Say

L	R
lice	rice
late	rate
light	right
lace	race
link	rink
belly	berry
bowl	bore

There are lice in the rice.
Rick clicked on the link.
Louie loves his Lincoln logs.

Larry licked a lollipop.
Rob lost his last race.
Laura loves Little Richard's lyrics.

I really like "Good Golly Miss Molly," "Lucille," and "Long Tall Sally."

For Fun   Little Boy Blue,
Come blow your horn,
The sheep's in the meadow,
The cow's in the corn;
Where is the boy
Who looks after the sheep?
Under the haystack
Fast asleep.
Will you wake him?
Oh no, not I,
For if I do
He will surely cry.

W

Consonants

P B		T D		K G
F V	th TH	S Z	CH J SH ZH	H
M		N		NG
W		L R		Y

Listen and Say

Once in a while	one way	one and only	once upon a time

Waste water   wishy washy
Worldwide   what in the world

Gene Wilder was Willy Wonka in a wonderful movie.
The Wicked Witch of the West was in *The Wizard of Oz*.

Once upon a time, they went out west in wagons. They wanted to wander the wilds. They walked in the woods. They watched wild animals. They went to the desert, where they wished for water.

Listen and Say

W	**V**
wary	very
wet	vet
we	vee
wine	vine
wail	vale
west	vest

For Fun

A weevil that lived in a pine
Tried to eat and survive in a vine.
    After tasting the grapes
    Of various shapes,
Said, "This'll make a very fine wine."

CD 2 ✳ **Track 18**   Y

P B			T D		K G
	F V	th TH	S Z	CH J SH ZH	H
M			N		NG
W			L R		**Y**

Consonants

Listen and Say

you   your yet young youth yell yawn yoke yucky

unit   universe uniform unique usual unite

union use useful Utah Utica U.S. Uruguay

For Fun

There was a young lady of Crewe
Who wanted to catch the two-oh-two.
    Said a porter, "Don't worry,
    Or hurry, or scurry –
It's a minute or two to two-oh-two."

A young man from old Yugoslavia
On his way to eat Caspian caviar,
    In Yalta he tarried,
    And there he was married.
And now on the Black Sea he's happier.

A young and unusual fellow,
A youth who was really quite mellow
    Grew yams in his yard
    That were not very hard
But as soft as bright yellow jello.

     77   *Photocopyable for classroom use.*

Consonant Clusters   CD 2 ✳ Track 19

A consonant cluster consists of two consonants that are said one after another. For example look at the word *pronounce*. It has the following sounds /PRONOUNS/. Notice that it begins with two consonants /PR/ and ends with two consonants /NS/. There are many consonant clusters in English. They can be at the beginning of a word, in the middle of a word, or at the end of a word. Most clusters are just two consonants, like the example above. However, there are some with three consonants, for example /STR/ as in /STREEM/.

Listen to and say these clusters and examples. Then write some.

/BL/	/KL/	/BR/	/KR/	/DR/	/FL/
blue	clue	brew	crew	drew	flew
black	clap	brash	crash	drag	flag
blow	cloak	broke	croak	droll	flow

/FR/	/GL/	/GR/	/PL/	/PR/	/KW/
fried	glide	grind	ply	pry	quite
free	glee	green	please	preen	queen
phrase	glaze	graze	plays	prays	quaint

/TR/	/SKR/	/STR/	/BL/	/KL/	/BR/
try	scribe	strive			
tree	scream	stream			
tray	scrape	stray			

/KR/	/DR/	/FL/	/FR/	/GL/	/GR/

/PL/	/PR/	/KW/	/TR/	/SKR/	/STR/

There are many final consonant clusters, especially with the final "s" and "ed" (see pages 63 and 66). Here are just a few others to practice.

/ST/	/ND/	/LD	/SK/	/MP/
last	land	bald	ask	lamp
feast	fiend	field	frisk	limp
bust	bend	held	tusk	bump

78

Syllables

A syllable can be a single sound (a vowel) or up to four or five sounds spoken as a unit. The core of the unit is a vowel and the other sounds are consonants. Here are some syllable patterns:

V	C-V	C-V-C	C-C-V-C	C-C-C-V-C	C-C-C-V-C-C
EE	T-EE	T-EE-M	S-T-EE-L	S-T-R-EE-K	S-T-R-E-NG-TH

Look at this list of words and write the words in the correct column. Column one is words of two syllables; column two has words with three syllables, and column three has four syllable words.

animal   lion   eagle giraffe scorpion ostrich   tiger
insect rhinoceros salamander dinosaur reptile octopus   rattlesnake
orangutan   gorilla chimpanzee leopard jaguar   beetle Gila monster
porcupine   beaver   butterfly   rabbit   hummingbird   spider
pelican   dolphin   elephant praying mantis   pheasant   anaconda
mongoose   giant squid   mountain lion   grizzly bear white-tailed sparrow

2 SYLLABLES   3 SYLLABLES   4 SYLLABLES

Answers on page 102.

After each name write the number of syllables in the entire name.
Example: Abraham Lincoln (5)

Mahatma Gandhi ( )   Queen Elizabeth ( )   Hillary Clinton ( )
Benazir Bhutto ( )   Winston Churchill ( )   Barack Obama ( )
Mikhail Gorbachev ( )   Desmond Tutu ( )   Mother Teresa ( )
Leo Tolstoy ( )   Simon Bolivar ( )   George Washington ( )
Orhan Pamuk ( )   Khaled Hosseini ( )   Naguib Mahfouz ( )
Nadine Gordimer ( )   Octavio Paz ( )   Toni Morrison ( )
Muhammad Yunus ( )   Wangari Maathai ( )   Jimmy Carter ( )
Mohamed ElBaradei ( )   Jody Williams ( )   Nelson Mandela ( )

Answers on page 102.

Stress

Syllable Stress 1 ● •

Pronounce the word *teacher*. The word has two syllables: *tea-* and *-cher*. The first syllable has is louder and a little longer than the second syllable: **tea** cher. This is called stress. The longer and louder sound of the first syllable is called PRIMARY stress and the shorter and quieter sound of second syllable is called SECONDARY.

Listen to these words. The first syllable has primary stress. It is printed in bold letters. The big circle represents primary stress. The smaller circle represents secondary stress.

● •	● •	● •
tea cher	**Mon** day	**morn** ing
Eng lish	**col** lege	**un** der
lec ture	**pa** per	**o** ver

Practice saying these names:

Albert	Francis	Kenneth	Paula	Victor
Betty	Georgia	Laura	Quentin	Walter
Carlos	Harold	Michael	Robert	Yuri
Donna	Ingrid	Nancy	Sandra	Zoey
Edward	Jason	Oden	Thomas	

Syllable Stress 2 • ●

Some words have primary stress on the second syllable. Listen to these words.

• ●	• ●	• ●
a **bove**	re **peat**	a **fraid**
re **turn**	al **low**	pre **tend**
sur **prise**	mis **take**	ap **pear**

There are no rules that are always true for stress, but we can make some general statements.

1. **Most** two-syllable words have primary stress on the first syllable.
2. Two-syllable words that have a prefix are **usually** pronounced with the primary stress on the second syllable.

Practice. Listen to these nonsense words and circle the syllable that has primary stress.

kinning	desack	kipful	pertrop
anoop	uggles	repalled	untock
gopply	vapy	kuster	fredded
prothorbed	tishken	affrond	norking
fribble	gulpin	imprale	sumpster

Answers on page 102.

CD 3 * Track 2 *Syllable Stress with nouns and verbs*

With some words, moving the primary stress from one syllable to the other can cause a change in the part of speech. A noun can become a verb and vice versa. There may also be a change in meaning.

Listen to these words. If the primary stress is on the first syllable, circle it and say "one." If it is on the second syllable, circle it and say "two."*

object	conduct	address
increase	produce	permit
contract	perfect	project

Which words are verbs?   Can you make a rule?

Answers on page 102.

Say these words as verbs:

subject	reject	record
conflict	address	decrease
convert	present	protest
rebel	contrast	extract
insult	progress	suspect
permit	refuse	desert
annex	conduct	

Now say them as nouns.

Say these sentences:

1. There are conflicting reports that the conflict may be over.

2. He converted to Islam last year. As a convert he now prays every day.

3. We can't permit you to do that. Your permit has expired.

4. She presented him with a beautiful present.

5. The dump refused to take the refuse because it was full.

6. The suspect addressed the jury and protested that he was not guilty.

7. They converted the annex into a shoe store.

8. The rebels rejected the peace plan.

9. Several soldiers deserted in the Western Desert.

* Teacher's note: hear answers for the pronunciation on the CD.

Syllable Stress with Three-Syllable Words

CD 3 * Track 3

Listen to these three-syllable words. Underline the syllable that has primary stress.
For example: <u>com</u>pany   after<u>noon</u>   pro<u>fes</u>sor

1. vacation	6. engineer	11. practicing
2. umbrella	7. lecturer	12. introduce
3. carefully	8. enemy	13. yesterday
4. seventy	9. allowance	14. remember
5. medicine	10. popular	15. contradict

Which words have primary stress on the first syllable?

Answers on page 103

Let's take a closer look at these words. Pronounce the word *animal*. It has three syllables:
an i mal. The first syllable has primary stress. The other two have WEAK stress. They
are very short and soft, and the vowels are often reduced to a short vowel called schwa.
In dictionaries it is represented with an upside down e, or /ə/.

Listen to and repeat these words. Give primary stress to the first syllable.

●··	●··	●··
animal	argument	chemistry
medicine	beautiful	furniture
Saturday	passenger	exercise
difficult	natural	ambulance
comfortable	generous	management
permanent	pitiful	poisonous
violent	capital	happiness

Now pronounce the word *tomorrow*. The word has three syllables *to mor row.*
The second (middle) syllable has primary stress. The other syllables have weak stress.

Listen to and repeat these words. Give primary stress to the second syllable.

·●·	·●·	·●·
adventure	important	remember
example	attractive	December
expensive	discover	repeated
mechanic	admission	convenient
advisor	attendance	computer
dictation	collection	confusion
profession	production	reflection

Continues on page 83

Pronounce the word *understand*. It has three syllables: *un der stand*. The third (last) syllable, *–stand*, has primary stress. The middle syllable, *-der-*, has weak stress. The first syllable, *un-* , has heavier stress than *-der-* but not as heavy as *-stand*. This is called SEC-ONDARY stress.

Listen to and repeat these words (with primary, secondary, and weak stress).

1	2	3
●.◐	●.◐	●.◐
overlook	introduce	interfere
disappoint	represent	insincere
interrupt	overwhelm	reappear
overwork	understand	afternooon
recommend		interact

Say sentences with the frame below and the words in columns 1 and 2.

They _____ ed her. (be careful with *understand*.)

Practice

Say these sentences with this pattern: •●•• •●•• •●••
The capital of Austria is beautiful.
The gentleman found happiness in Germany.
The photographs of Italy are colorful.
The calendar from Mexico is wonderful.

Say this poem: (The first verse of *Jabberwocky* by Lewis Carroll)

'Twas brillig and the slithy toves
    Did gyre and gimble in the wabe;
All mimsy were the borogoves,
    And the mome raths outgrabe.

Listen and underline any secondary stresses.

Vermont	Massachusetts	Rhode Island	Connecticut
New Hampshire	Pennsylvania	Delaware	Maryland
West Virginia	North Carolina	Georgia	Florida
Alabama	Mississippi	Tennessee	Kentucky
Michigan	Ohio	Indiana	Illinois
Wisconsin	Missouri	Arkansas	Louisiana
Texas	Oklahoma	Kansas	Nebraska
South Dakota	New Mexico	Colorado	Wyoming
Montana	Idaho	Utah	Arizona
California	Washington	Alaska	Hawaii

Answers on page 103.

                       Photocopyable for classroom use.

Vowel reduction CD 3 * Track 4

In multi-syllable words, when one syllable receives primary stress, the vowel of the other syllables may receive secondary stress or weak stress. Listen to these words and notice the stress patterns.

pronoun
pronounce
mispronounce
pronunciation

Notice how the weakly stressed vowels tend to collapse and become hard to hear, and without any clear vowel sound. This is called vowel reduction and it is very common in English, especially when several words are said as a phrase. The reduced vowel is a quiet vowel like /I /or a quiet version of /UH/, which we will note with /uh/.

In general, when a suffix is added to a word, the primary stress does not move to another syllable. Listen to and say these pairs.

help/helpful	trouble/troublesome	care/careless
real/realize	work/worker	fame/famous
accept/acceptable	type/typist	second/secondary
govern/government	port/portable	happy/happiness

However, if the suffix is *-ion, -ic, -ity, -acy*, the stress often moves. Listen to these multi-syllable words. Then try saying them yourself.

classify/classification	metal/metallic	human/humanity
qualify/qualification	meter/metric	active/activity
diversify/diversification	drama/dramatic	equal/equality
clarify /clarification	opera/operatic	similar/similarity
verify/verification	telephone/telephonic	relative/relativity
identify/identification	magnet/magnetic	democrat/democracy

In which word did the stress not move?

When words are part of a phrase, it is common for the most important word in that phrase (usually a noun, verb, adjective, or adverb) to "steal" all the stress and leave the other words with weak stress and reduced vowels.

Listen to and say these phrases.

Because of the weather   the flight to Houston   has been delayed.
The two of us   saw him   in the garden   picking some lowers.
One of the boys   climbed up a tree   and stole some eggs   from a bird's nest.
If you want to go to the concert   with Jenny and Jim,   you'd better
        get your ticket now.

CD 3 ✳ Track 5  *Sentence Stress*

Pronounce *teacher*. Pronounce *busy*. Both these words have a primary-weak stress pattern. Notice what happens when these words are spoken as part of a sentence.

teacher busy   The teacher is busy.

The final word, *busy*, still has primary-weak stress. But *bus-* has a stronger stress than *teach-*. Let's call it SENTENCE FINAL STRESS or maybe "super primary," and mark it with ● .

Listen to and repeat these words and sentences.

baby   crying   The baby is crying.
doctor speaking   The doctor is speaking.
children naughty   The children were naughty.

studying English   We are studying English.

Sentence stress, unless there is some other reason (such as emphatic stress), usually falls on the last primary stressed syllable at the end of the sentence. This use of stress is also a signal to the listener that a statement has been completed, and if appropriate, the listener may now respond.

Practice

Mark these sentences for secondary, primary, and sentence final stress.

1. We had a nice vacation on Cape Cod.

2. She's never been to Washington, D.C.

3. New Orleans is famous for its French cuisine.

4. Seattle is the largest city in the state of Washington.

5. I have been to the Sawtooth Mountains in Idaho several times.

6. Nogales, Arizona shares the international border with Nogales, Mexico.

7. Niagara Falls and the Great Lakes are shared by the U.S. and Canada.

8. The Bay of Fundy is the body of water between New Brunswick and Nova Scotia.

Answers on page 103.

Emphatic Stress   CD 3 ✳ Track 6

Often we give one word in a sentence more stress than usual in order to emphasize one idea in contrast to another. Repeat each of the following sentences. Stress the underlined word. Note the change in meaning.

Sentence	**Meaning**
<u>Paul</u> bought a ball.	Not Peter, John, or Bill; it was <u>Paul</u>.
Paul <u>bought</u> a ball.	Not lost, sold, or stole it; he <u>bought</u> it.
Paul bought a <u>ball</u>.	Not a book, bowl, or bicycle; it was a <u>ball</u>.

Practice. Listen to and repeat the following sentences.

A. I don't know what you <u>mean</u>.

B. I don't know what <u>you</u> mean.

C. I don't know <u>what</u> you mean.

D. I don't <u>know</u> what you mean.

E. I <u>don't</u> know what you mean.

F. <u>I</u> don't know what you mean.

What does each of these sentences mean? Talk about it.

Say this sentence with the meaning that is contrasted by each of the following statements.

Yoshi speaks Spanish very well.

1. It isn't Hamed.

2. He doesn't read it.

3. He doesn't speak Turkish.

4. He doesn't speak poorly.

5. It isn't Yuko.

6. He doesn't speak French.

7. He doesn't write it.

8. He doesn't speak Arabic.

CD 3 ✳ Track 7 *Pitch and Intonation*

1. Sing the first line of "Row, row, row your boat." Your voice goes higher as you sing the last two words.

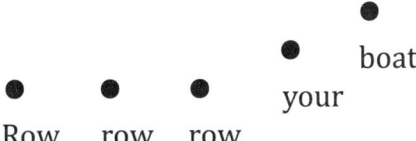

The difference between the height of these words is a difference of pitch. *Boat* is sung on a higher pitch than *your*; *your* is is sung higher than *row*.

Now "sing" the words in these three columns.

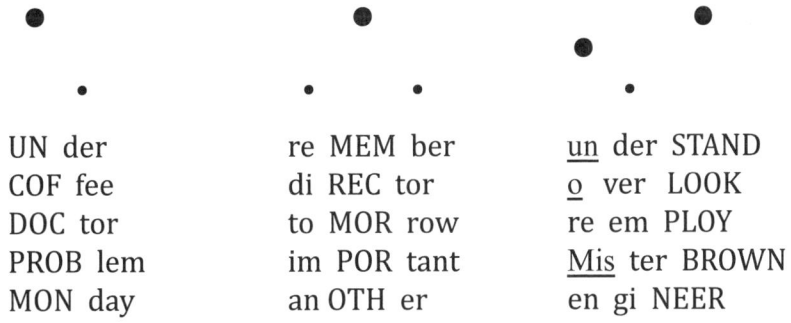

UN der	re MEM ber	<u>un</u> der STAND
COF fee	di REC tor	<u>o</u> ver LOOK
DOC tor	to MOR row	re em PLOY
PROB lem	im POR tant	<u>Mis</u> ter BROWN
MON day	an OTH er	en gi NEER

2. Stress and pitch tend to go together. Usually the syllable with the primary stress is pronounced on a higher pitch than the other syllables. We will call these pitch levels HIGH, MID, and LOW.

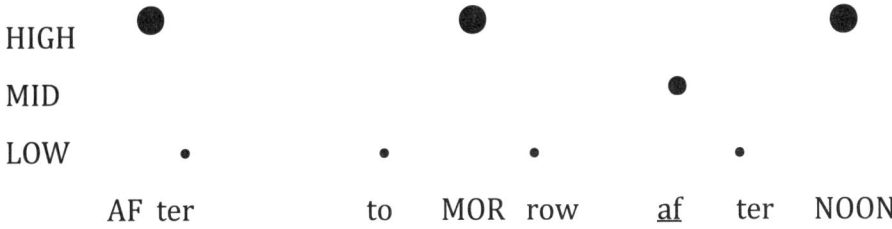

3. Now listen to these three sentences.

   1. She's a teacher.
   2. She's a teacher . . .
   3. She's a teacher ?

The first sentence ends on a LOW pitch. It is a statement. It has a period at the end.
The second sentence ends on a MID pitch. It is an incomplete statement. We expect the speaker to continue, to say something more.
The third sentence ends on a HIGH pitch. It is a question. It has a question mark at the end.

4. Listen to these sentences. Decide if the final pitch is HIGH, MID, or LOW. Mark H, M, or L in the box. Each sentence will be said five times.*

	1	2	3	4	5
She's a very good doctor	L	H	L	M	H
You don't understand					
The dictionary is lost					
They're from Australia					
Vermont is a beautiful state					

5. Practice saying these sentences. First decide whether you will say a statement, an incomplete statement, or a question. After you say your sentence, ask someone to tell you whether it was a statement, an incomplete statement, or a question.

1. Haste makes waste.
2. Don't judge a book by its cover.
3. Too many cooks spoil the broth.
4. Silence is golden.
5. A watched pot never boils.

As stress and pitch tend to go together, when sentences are spoken, the rise and fall of the voice is called the INTONATION of the sentence. Listen to this sentence.

Eight countries have a coastline on the Persian Gulf and the Gulf of Oman.

Which syllables have the strongest stress and mid or high pitch? As a simple statement of fact, most people would probably have HIGH or MID pitch on these syllables:

Eight   coun   coast   Per   Gulf   Gulf   man

Now look at the full intonation of the sentence.

H
M
L Eight coun tries have a coast line on the Per sian Gulf and the Gulf of O ma an

People may actually say this sentence in slightly different ways, but the important points to notice are that intonation follows stress and rises and falls through the sentence until the very end, where it may rise for a question or fall for a statement.

And notice that in a statement when the final syllable has the sentence final stress, the intonation dives down through the final syllable: O MAan

* Teacher's note. The first sentence is marked according to the CD.

CD 3 * Track 8   *Intonation of Questions*

Notice the difference in intonation of these two questions, and the different kind of answer to each question.

1. Are you a student?   Yes.

2. Where are you studying?   Here.

The first question expects the answer to be *yes* or *no*; therefore, it is called a **yes/no question.** Questions of this kind are usually said with a rising intonation. They end on a high pitch.

Examples of yes/no questions:

Is he from Venezuela?

Can he speak Portuguese?

Didn't he study in Brazil?

Does he like baseball?

The second question asks for information; therefore it is called an **information question.** Questions of this kind cannot be answered with *yes* or *no*; they require more information and words. Information questions are usually spoken with a falling intonation.

Examples of information questions:

Who can speak Swahili?

What is the capital of Kenya?

When will you go there?

Where is it spoken?

How do you know?

Why are you going?

Write some questions that you would like to ask someone in your class. Write yes/no and information questions. Then ask your questions, and ask your partner if your intonation rises or falls, and if it is correct.

And remember that when the final syllable is a primary stressed syllable, the intonation glides through the syllable; but if the final syllable doesn't have primary stress, the intonation falls between the syllables:

What's your name?

Where is my dictionary?

How did you find it?

Why are you studying English?

When did you lose it?

Who has my pronunciation book?

Contrastive Intonation   CD 3 ✷ **Track 9**

A sentence may include a contrast or difference between two parts of the sentence. For example, listen to these sentences:

> Is tennis easier than golf?
> Which do you prefer, American football or soccer?
> Are the Red Sox better than the Yankees?
> A basketball is bigger than a soccer ball.
> I'll take the metro rather than the bus.
> Do you want coffee or tea?
> My brother likes the Giants, but I like the Dodgers. (double contrast)

The intonation pattern and stress follow the two items that are being contrasted.

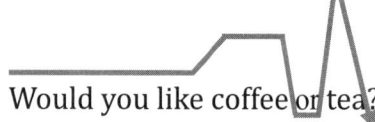

Would you like coffee or tea?

Notice the different intonation when the two items are not being contrasted.

Would you like coffee or tea?

What's the difference in meaning?

Say these sentences.

> Which is bigger, Boston or San Francisco?
> Buffalo is in western New York, whereas Albany is in eastern New York.
> I think he lives in either Minneapolis or St. Paul.
> Miami is further south than Dallas.
> Kentucky is slightly larger than Indiana.
> Is Phoenix farther north than Tucson?
> I know that Alaska is much bigger than Texas.
> Where would you rather live, Colorado or Wyoming?

Now make your own contrastive sentences with these words.

newspaper - magazine	book - digital reader	book - audiobook
television - radio	MAC - PC	cinema - theater
dramas - comedies	talk shows - evening news	pop music - classical
texting - talking	fiction - nonfiction	guitar - piano

       Photocopyable for classroom use.

CD 3 ✳ Track 10	*Linking*

Try to say this sentence, *I want a easy answer.* Do you notice that it is not easy to say *a easy*? Why? When one word ends with a vowel and the next begins with a vowel, it will be much easier to put a consonant between the two vowels. That is why we have *a* and *an.*

Listen to and say these phrases. Notice how the words are linked together.

an easy answer	an eager actor	an absent owner
an early evening	an awful error	an angry artist
an extra office	an unusual answer	an apple a day

Did you notice that the words are pronounced smoothly together without any "space" between them? The final /N/ consonant sound flows smoothly into the following vowel sound.

Substitute the following words into this sentence. Link the words together smoothly. I will give the first one. It's an _____apple_____ .

a) apple	b) alarm	c) animal	d) adventure
oven	attack	accident	election
island	escape	Indian	expression
orange	excuse	instrument	invention
arrow	amount	elephant	advantage
echo	ideal	article	occasion

Now listen to these phrases.

the new book	the old book
the big apple	the only apple
the fat cat	the awful cat

Did you notice that *the* before a consonant is pronounced with the vowel /uh/, but before a vowel sound it is pronounced with the /EE/ sound and then links very easily with the following vowel sound. Try these phrases.

the page	the age	the game	the aim
the leg	the egg	the lake	the ache
the box	the ox	the feast	the east
the soil	the oil	the tax	the axe
the rice	the ice	the shade	the aid

Continues on page 92

Linking - 2

Now notice these phrases:

three apples	stay open	my uncle	how often
who asked	grow old	sea eagle	fly above
New England	how active	who knew	be aware

Words that end with a vowel sound are almost always the longer vowel that actually ends with a /Y/ or /W/: EE, AI, AW, AY, UW, OW, OY .

A very common link occurs when a word ends with a consonant sound and the next word begins with a vowel sound. Listen to and say these phrases

drop over	rub off	put away	pick up	beg off
laugh about	drive over	breathe easy	both answers	work out
close up	raise up	wash up	catch up	urge on
come up	run up	ring up	call up	tear up

Practice

1. Pronounce these sentences with the same stress and rhythm. Link all the words together smoothly.

It's an

official argument.
enormous elephant.
expensive ornament.
important exercise.
essential article.

2. Say these sentences.

The answer is easy.	The oven is open.
The actor is absent.	The engines are useful.
The opera is over.	The authors are angry.
The autumn is early.	The uncles are early.

3. Say or sing this song.

We went to the animal fair.
The birds and the beasts were there.
The big baboon by the light of the moon
Was combing his auburn hair.
The monkey he got drunk.
He sat on the elephant's trunk.
The elephant sneezed
Fell down on his knees
And that was the end of the monk.

92

CD 3 ✳ Track 11	*Phrasing*

When we carry on a conversation, tell a story, give a report, or make a speech, our sentences are spoken as groups of words (phrases), many of them linked together. In other words, a sentence, especially a long one, is naturally delivered with pauses, some very, very brief. At the same time, the important words in phrases are stressed, and the intonation usually rises with stresses and falls at the pauses. This helps listeners focus on the meanings of the parts of our sentence as we speak. In the passage below, break the sentences up into smaller pieces using slash marks (/). The first two sentences are done.

One of the most influential families/ in American politics/ is the Kennedy family./ John F. Kennedy,/ 35ᵗʰ President /of the U.S.,/ was the great-grandson/ of Patrick Kennedy, /who came to America/ from Ireland/ in 1840./ Patrick was a penniless farmer,/who settled in Boston,/Massachusetts,/where many Irish/ had settled.

John F. Kennedy's father, Joseph, was a self-made millionaire. He and his wife, Rose, had nine children. The parents raised their children in a close, but strict, Catholic family. They taught the children loyalty and duty to the family. Family always came first in everything they did. And all were expected to succeed.

The family spent its summers on Cape Cod in a huge summer home where the children swam, sailed, and lived a privileged life. Politics was often the main topic at the dinner table. When John ran for President, the whole family campaigned actively: mother, father, brothers, sisters, even in-laws. It was a family effort, and John won.

The country was fascinated with the young couple who occupied the White House with their two small children. Tragically, John was assassinated while in office. It was a huge loss for the nation.*

*Adapted from *Plays for the Holidays*, by Anne Siebert, Pro Lingua Associates, 2006.

Answers on page 104.

Phrasing - 2　　　　　CD 3 * Track 12

On this page from "The Kennedys: An Immigrant Success Story,"* mark the phrase groups with a slash (/). Then, with your classmates, read it dramatically.

Narrator:　　It's dinner time at the Kennedy home. The children are busy eating and talking. Now Joe, Jr. speaks rudely to John, his younger brother, whom everyone calls Jack.

Joe, Jr.:　　Jack, pass the potatoes! You can't have them all!

Mother:　　Hush now, Joe! Where are your manners? Ask nicely, and you will get them.

Joe, Jr.:　　Jack, would you PLEASE pass the potatoes.

John:　　Here you are, SIR.

Father:　　So children, what did you read in the newspaper today?

John:　　I read something about the economic depression. Dad, what do you think of President Roosevelt's policies? Do you think he's doing a good job?

Father:　　It looks that way, Jack. But a lot of people are out of work. In this depression, many people have no jobs, and there are no jobs for them.

Joe, Jr.:　　If I were President, I'd make sure everyone had a job. That's what I'd do!

Father:　　Joe, someday you will be President. Why not? In America, anyone can be President, if they set their mind to it, even if they're Irish.

*Adapted from *Plays for the Holidays*, by Anne Siebert, Pro Lingua Associates, 2006.

Answers on page 105.

CD 3 ✳ **Track 13**	*Rhythm*

Listen to these words and phrases, and then say them. Notice that each phrase has two stressed syllables but a different number of unstressed syllables.

	●		●
	speak		French
	speak	some	French
They	speak	some	French
They can	speak	some	French
They can	speak	a little	French

Did you notice that it takes almost the same amount of time to say each phrase, but the number of syllables in each phrase increases from top to bottom. And the unstressed syllables are said very quickly. This is called the stress-timed rhythm of English. Practice English rhythm with this song. Say it or sing it with four beats (stresses) to the line.

This Old Man

This old man, he played one,
He played nick-nack on my thumb,
With a nick-nack paddy whack, give a dog a bone,
This old man came rolling home.

This old man, he played two,
He played nick-nack on my shoe,
With a nick-nack paddy whack, give a dog a bone,
This old man came rolling home.

This old man, he played three,
He played nick-nack on my knee,
With a nick-nack paddy whack, give a dog a bone,
This old man came rolling home.

. . . four . . . on my door	. . . eight . . . on my gate
. . . five . . . on my hive	. . . nine . . . on my spine
. . . six . . . on my sticks	. . . ten . . . once again
. . . seven. . . up in heaven	

Limericks for Practice

CD 3 ✳ Track 14

A flea and a fly in a flue
Were imprisoned, so what could they do?
　　　Said the fly, "Let us flee!"
　　　Said the flea, "Let us fly!"
So they flew through a flaw in the flue.

There once was a spaceman named Wright,
Whose speed was much faster than light.
　　　He set out one day
　　　In a relative way
And returned on the previous night!

A young rock-and-roller named Clyde
Always kept his guitar by his side.
　　　All night he was strumming
　　　And never stopped humming
Till he ran out of rhythm and died.

God's plan had a hopeful beginning,
But man spoiled his chances by sinning.
　　　We hope that the story
　　　Will end in God's glory –
But at present, the other side's winning.

An old maid, a foolish romantic,
Said as she crossed the Atlantic,
　　　"Now is my chance
　　　To find true romance
On this beautiful ship the Titanic."

I wish that my room had a floor.
I don't care as much for a door.
　　　But this walking around
　　　Without touching the ground
Is getting to be quite a bore.

There was a young man from Japan
Who wrote verse that never would scan.
　　　When they said, "But the thing
　　　Doesn't go with a swing,"
He said, "Yes, but I always like to get as many
　　　words into the last line as I possibly can."

Appendix

Pronunciation Problem Areas for Selected Learners

Vowels.

Virtually all learners will have difficulty distinguishing the /EE/I/ and the /E/A/ vowel contrasts. Many will also have difficulty with the lower vowels: /A/AH/UH/AW/, and the back vowels /U/UW/. Other vowel problem areas are noted in the list below.

Consonants.

Very few languages use /th ~ TH/, therefore these sounds are troublesome for all. Otherwise, language-specific consonant problems are listed below.

Arabic:	E/I	P/B	F/V		
Chinese:	A/E	L/N	L/W	R/W/L	W/V
Czech:	E/A	W/V	th/T	D/th	W/V
Farsi:	W/V	R			
French:	CH/J	R	H		
German:	O	W/V	R		
Greek:	S/SH	S/Z	R	H	
Hindi:	E/A	F/P	V/B	W/V	
Italian:	H	R			
Japanese:	S/SH	T/CH	B/V	L/R	
Korean:	P/F	B/V	S/SH	L/R	
Polish:	W/V	L/W	R	NG	
Portuguese:	SH/CH	J/ZH	S/SH	L/W	
Russian:	E/A	ER	W	NG	
Serbo-Croatian:	E/A	W/V			
Spanish:	B/V	CH/SH	J/Y	S/Z	R
Thai:	I/E	AI/E	P/F	W/V	SH/CH	L/R
Turkish:	E/A	V/W			
Vietnamese:	E/A	P/F/B			

A Comparison of Three Phonetic Alphabets

Vowels

Sounds	I.P.A.*	This book	Dict.**
beat	/i/	/EE/	i: / ij
bit	/ɪ/	/I/	I
bait	/e/	/AI/	eɪ / ej
bet	/ɛ/	/E/	ɛ
bat	/æ/	/A/	æ
her	/ɚ/	/ER/	ɚ
but	/ʌ/	/UH/	ʌ
alone	/ə/	/uh/	ə
boot	/u/	/OO/	u: / u:w
put	/ʊ/	/U/	ʊ
boat	/o/	/O/	oʊ / ow
bought	/ɔ/	/AW/	a:
pot	/ɑ/	/AU/	a:
how	/aʊ/	/OU/	aʊ / aw
I	/aɪ/	/AY/	aɪ / aj
boy	/ɔɪ/	/OY/	oi/oj

*International Phonetic Alphabet
**Merriam-Webster Advanced Learner's Dictionary

99

Consonants

Sounds   **Representations**

	I.P.A.*	This book	Dict.**
may	/m/	/M/	m
bay	/b/	/B/	b
pay	/p/	/P/	p
way	/w/	/W/	w
whey	/hw/	/HW/	hw
vee	/v/	/V/	v
fee	/f/	/F/	f
thee	/ð/	/TH/	ð
thigh	/θ/	/th/	θ
new	/n/	/N/	n
dew	/d/	/D/	d
too	/t/	/T/	t
Lou	/l/	/L/	l
zoo	/z/	/Z/	z
Sue	/s/	/S/	s
you	/j/	/Y/	j
rue	/r/	/R/	r
measure	/ʒ/	/ZH/	ʒ
show	/ʃ/	/SH/	ʃ
joke	/dʒ/	/J/	dʒ
choo	/tʃ/	/CH/	tʃ
bang	/ŋ/	/NG/	ŋ
bag	/g/	/G/	g
back	/k/	/K/	k
hi	/h/	/H/	h

*International Phonetic Alphabet
**Merriam-Webster Advanced Learner's Dictionary

Answers

Page

3. *Bit* and *feet* and *Will* and *weak* are not minimal pairs.

5. Other /AI/ spellings:
   ay as in *day*
   ea as in *great*
   ei as in *weigh*
   ey as in *they*

24. Texts /TEKSTS/   worlds /WERLDZ/

25. ____ review   re view   CV CCV
    ____ column   col umn   CVC VC
    ____ headline   head line   CVC CVC
    ____ newspaper   news pa per   CVC CV CV
    ____ editorial   ed i tor i al   VC V CVC V VC
    ____ opinion   o pin ion   V CVC CVC
    ____ classified   class i fied   CCVC V CVC
    ____ political   po lit i cal   CV CVC V CVC
    ____ accident   ac ci dent   VC CV CVCC
    ____ international   in ter na tion al   VC CV CV CVC VC
    ____ information   in for ma tion VC CVC CV CVC
    ____ advertisement ad ver tise ment VC CV CVC CVCC

26.   <u>Bos</u> ton   constit<u>u</u>tion
      <u>Cleve</u> land   decl<u>a</u>ration
      On   <u>tar</u> i   o   <u>a</u>mend<u>m</u>ent
      Ne   <u>bras</u> ka   cap<u>i</u>talism
      Los <u>An</u>   gel   es   repr<u>e</u>sent<u>a</u>tive
      Min ne   <u>ap</u>   o   lis   c<u>o</u>ngress<u>io</u>nal
      Phil a   <u>del</u> phi   a

28.
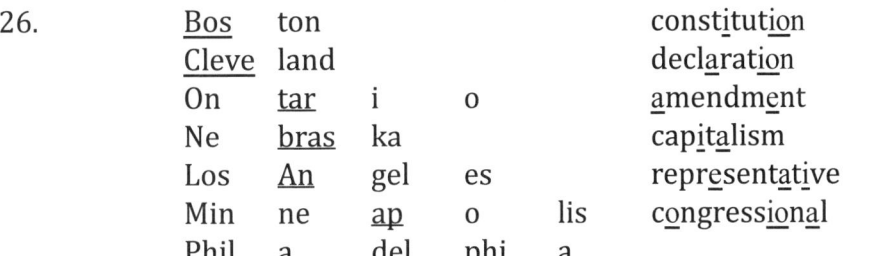

Individual   complicated   problematic   suprasegmental

Nevertheless   secondary   interpretation   intonation

101

31.

● ● .● . ● . . ●
● ●

/AY BAWT uhNAPL uhNAWRuhNJ uhNDuhNUHNYuhN/

79.

Two Syllables	Three Syllables	Four Syllables
insect	animal	orangutan
mongoose	porcupine	rhinoceros
lion	pelican	salamander
beaver	gorilla	mountain lion
dolphin	giant squid	praying mantis
eagle	chimpanzee	white-tailed sparrow
giraffe	butterfly	Gila monster
leopard	elephant	anaconda
rabbit	dinosaur	
reptile	grizzly bear	
jaguar	scorpion	
ostrich	octopus	
beetle	hummingbird	
pheasant	rattlesnake	
tiger		
spider		

79.

Mahatma Gandhi (5)	Queen Elizabeth (5)	Hillary Clinton (5)
Benazir Bhutto (5)	Winston Churchill (4)	Barack Obama (5)
Mikhail Gorbachev (5)	Desmond Tutu (4)	Mother Teresa (5)
Leo Tolstoy (4)	Simon Bolivar (5)	George Washington (4)
Orhan Pamuk (4)	Khaled Hosseini (5)	Naguib Mahfouz (4)
Nadine Gordimer (5)	Octavio Paz (5)	Toni Morrison (5)
Muhammad Yunus (5)	Wangari Maathai (5)	Jimmy Carter (4)
Mohamed ElBaradei (7)	Jody Williams (4)	Nelson Mandela (5)

80.

kinning	desack	kipful	pertrop
anoop	uggles	repalled	untock
gopply	vapy	kuster	fredded
prothorbed	tishken	affrond	norking
fribble	gulpin	imprale	sumpster

81.

object	conduct	address
increase	produce	permit
contract	perfect	project

82.
1. vacation
2. umbrella
3. carefully
4. seventy
5. medicine
6. engineer
7. lecturer
8. enemy
9. allowance
10. popular
11. practicing
12. introduce
13. yesterday
14. remember
15. contradict

83.
Vermont
New Hampshire
West Virginia
Alabama
Michigan
Wisconsin
Texas
South Dakota
Montana
California

Massachusetts
Pennsylvania
North Carolina
Mississippi
Ohio
Missouri
Oklahoma
New Mexico
Idaho
Washington

Rhode Island
Delaware
Georgia
Tennessee
Indiana
Arkansas
Kansas
Colorado
Utah
Alaska

Connecticut
Maryland
Florida
Kentucky
Illinois
Louisiana
Nebraska
Wyoming
Arizona
Hawaii

85.
1. We had a nice vacation on Cape Cod.

2. She's never been to Washington, D. C.

3. New Orleans is famous for its French cuisine.

4. Seattle is the largest city in the state of Washington.

5. I have been to the Sawtooth Mountains in Idaho several times.

6. Nogales, Arizona shares the international border with Nogales, Mexico.

7. Niagara Falls and the Great Lakes are shared by the U.S. and Canada.

8. The Bay of Fundy is the body of water between New Brunswick and Nova Scotia.

93.   One of the most influential families/ in American politics/ is the Kennedy
       family./ John F. Kennedy,/ 35th President /of the U.S.,/ was the great-grandson/
       of Patrick Kennedy, /who came to America/ from Ireland/ in 1840./ Patrick was
       a penniless farmer,/who settled in Boston,/Massachusetts,/ where many Irish/
       had settled.

       John F. Kennedy's father,/ Joseph, /was a self-made millionaire./ He and his
       wife,/ Rose,/ had nine children./ The parents raised their children/ in a close,/
       but strict,/ Catholic family./ They taught the children/ loyalty and duty/ to the
       family./ Family/ always came first/ in everything they did./ And all were
       expected/ to succeed.

       The family/ spent its summers/ on Cape Cod/ in a huge summer home/ where
       the children swam,/ sailed,/ and lived a privileged life./ Politics/ was often the
       main topic,/ at the dinner table./ When John ran for President,/ the whole
       family/ campaigned actively:/ mother,/ father,/ brothers,/ sisters,/ even
       in-laws./ It was a family effort,/ and John won.

       The country was fascinated with the young couple/ who occupied the White
       House/ with their two small children./ Tragically,/ John was assassinated/ while
       in office./ It was a huge loss/ for the nation.*

     *Adapted from *Plays for the Holidays*, by Anne Siebert, Pro Lingua Associates, 2006.

94.

Narrator: It's dinner time/ at the Kennedy home./ The children/ are busy eating and talking./ Now Joe, Jr./ speaks rudely/ to John,/ his younger brother,/ whom everyone calls/ Jack.

Joe, Jr.: Jack,/ pass the potatoes!/ You can't have them all!

Mother: Hush now, Joe!/ Where are your manners?/ Ask nicely,/ and you will get them.

Joe, Jr.: Jack,/ would you PLEASE/ pass the potatoes.

John: Here you are,/ SIR.

Father: So children,/ what did you read/ in the newspaper today?

John: I read something/ about the economic depression./ Dad,/ what do you think/of President Roosevelt's policies?/ Do you think/ he's doing a good job?

Father: It looks that way,/ Jack./ But a lot of people/are out of work./ In this depression,/ many people/ have no jobs,/ and there are no jobs/ for them.

Joe, Jr.: If I were President,/ I'd make sure/ everyone had a job./ That's what I'd do!

Father: Joe,/ someday you will be President./ Why not?/ In America,/ anyone can be President,/ if they set their mind to it,/ even if they're Irish.

*Adapted from *Plays for the Holidays*, by Anne Siebert, Pro Lingua Associates, 2006.

Other Pronunciation Books from Pro Lingua

Pronunciation Card Games

Easy game activities help learners practice and learn the sounds and "melody" of English. There are 16 photocopyable sets of game cards which help learners improve both production and discrimination of individual sounds (segmentals) and stress, reduction, and emphatic stress (suprasegmentals).

Pronunciation Activities

Pronunciation practice is made fun and effective with 16 units featuring the vowels. Each unit begins with a comical limerick about a character (the front vowels are Rita, Billy, Edna, Amy, and Adam) illustrated in a witty cartoon, and goes on to a variety of activities featuring the vowel. A CD of the limericks and other readings is available.

Rhymes 'n Rhythms

Thirty-two rhymes to read aloud, chant chorally, or listen to. They progress from short and easy rhymes that focus on questions, places, and times to longer and lexically more challenging verses on topics such as color, clothing, the body, occupations, and food. In addition to being an excellent way to work on stress, rhythm, and intonation, the rhymes are enjoyable – light, catchy, and playful. A CD with four different voices is available.

Stress Rulz!

Pronunciation through rap! This is pronunciation practice focused on the key feature of English pronunciation: stress. The stress-timed rhythm of English is a challenge to many learners whose languages do not use this system. So learning the rules of stress can dramatically improve overall speaking and comprehension. And this photocopyable booklet with its accompanying CD makes learning about stress fun. A free User Guide is also available.

From Sound to Sentence

Learning to Read and Write English. This basic literacy book uses a phonics approach supplemented with sight words. Five vowels and consonants are used in the first unit to practice sound-letter correspondence. Each succeeding unit adds more sound-letter pairs and spelling variations, and at the same time culminates in light and easy reading passages that get longer and more complex – and are still fun. Recordings on three CDs provide modeling and listening/pronunciation practice.

Superphonic Bingo

Breaking the Sounds Barrier. This is phonics practice as an enjoyable learning experience. There are 15 photocoyable games, each game with 8 different cards and two incomplete cards for "do it yourself." The games proceed from simple and easy to challenging. Game 1 uses 5 short vowels and consonants, and game 15 uses all vowels and consonants.

For more information or to order, visit www.ProLinguaAssociates.com
or call our hotline, 800-366-4775.